DAY HIKES ON THE
California
Southern
Coast

100 GREAT HIKES

Robert Stone

D1502647

Day Hike Books, Inc.
RED LODGE, MONTANA

Published by Day Hike Books, Inc.
P.O. Box 865
Red Lodge, Montana 59068

Distributed by The Globe Pequot Press
246 Goose Lane
P.O. Box 480
Guilford, CT 06437-0480
800-243-0495 (direct order) · 800-820-2329 (fax order)
www.globe-pequot.com

Photographs by Robert Stone
Design by Paula Doherty

The author has made every attempt to provide accurate information
in this book. However, trail routes and features may change—please
use common sense and forethought, and be mindful of your own
capabilities. Let this book guide you, but be aware that each hiker
assumes responsibility for their own safety. The author and publisher
do not assume any responsibility for loss, damage, or injury caused
through the use of this book.

Cover photo: Torrey Pines State Reserve, page 174.
Back cover photo: Sunset Cliffs Park, page 208.

Table of Contents

THE HIKES

Ventura County

Los Angeles County

Orange County

North San Diego County

South San Diego County

Southern California Coastal Area

The southern California coast has some of the most diverse and scenic geography in the state. These 100 day hikes are found along 238 miles of coastline through the southern-most counties of Ventura, Los Angeles, Orange, and San Diego. The hikes include a vast majority of the beach communities, lagoons, estuaries, piers, state beaches, and parks along or near the Pacific Ocean.

Despite the development of southern California, there are hundreds of miles of trails throughout scenic public lands and preserves. Highlights include sandy beaches, marine terraces, rocky headlands, tidal estuaries ideal for exploring, bay-side coves, sandstone cliffs, caves, wildlife observation sites, light-houses, expansive dunes, forested canyons, waterfalls, and panoramic oceanfront overlooks.

An overall map on page 10 identifies the general locations of the hikes and major access roads of the four counties. Individual county maps, as noted on this map, provide additional details.

Each hike includes its own map, a summary, driving and hiking directions, and an overview of distance/time/elevation. Relevant maps, including U.S.G.S. topographic maps, are listed with each hike to further explore the area. A quick glance at the hikes' summaries will help you choose a hike that is appropriate to your ability and desire.

A few basic necessities will make hiking more enjoyable. Wear supportive, comfortable hiking shoes. Take along hats, sunscreen, sunglasses, drinking water, snacks, and appropriate outerwear. Poison oak and ticks are common. Exercise caution by using insect repellent and staying on the trails.

Ventura County

Hikes 1—16 are located in Ventura County. The hikes are within a short distance of Ventura and Oxnard, yet offer solitude and beauty along protected stretches of coastline, rolling sand dunes, and mountain canyons.

Thousands of acres of public land and an impressive series of state parks are found between Ventura and Los Angeles in the Santa Monica Mountains. Hikes 10—15 travel across this mountain range through Point Mugu State Park, Rancho Sierra Vista/Satwiwa, and Circle X Ranch.

Among the best hikes are the Big Sycamore Canyon Trail (Hike 10), a one-way mountains-to-the-sea journey down a beautiful canyon, and the Grotto Trail, meandering through a maze of volcanic boulders in a narrow gorge (Hike 14).

Los Angeles County

Hikes 17—48 are located in Los Angeles County. Continuing along the Santa Monica Mountains are Hikes 17—32, which follow the Pacific Coast through foothills, canyons, and peaks. The Santa Monica Mountains extend roughly 46 miles east and west parallel to the coast, from downtown Los Angeles to Point Mugu in Ventura County. The mountains are 8—12 miles wide and lie along the San Andreas Fault. Elevations range from sea level to 3,111 feet at Sandstone Peak (Hike 16).

Highlights of the hikes include panoramic views from the ocean to the city, unusual geological formations, waterfalls, cliff overlooks, canyons, old ranch roads, and shady retreats. Los Angeles County's better known state parks include Leo Carrillo, Zuma/Trancas Canyons, Malibu Creek, and Topanga. Hikes are scattered amidst the beaches and coastal communities along the Pacific Coast Highway (Highway 1), the access road to all of these hikes.

Hikes 33—38 explore the oceanfront and interesting culture along Santa Monica Bay. A continuous series of ocean-side paths and boardwalks connect the beaches along the bay, from Santa Monica to Marina Del Rey (including Venice Beach).

Hikes 40—47 lie around the perimeter of the Palos Verdes Peninsula at the southernmost point of Los Angeles County. This geographically interesting area includes oceanside cliffs, beaches, coves, actively slipping landslides, and some of the best tidepools in the area. A beautiful lighthouse sits at the tip of Point Fermin (Hike 46). Sunken City, also at Point Fermin, is a surreal uninhabited landscape of house foundations and chimneys that continue to slide closer to the ocean (Hike 47).

Orange County

Hikes 49—66 are located in Orange County, between the large Los Angeles and San Diego counties. The coastline ranges from wide, flat, sandy beaches near Long Beach, at the north end, to the hilly bluff coast at the San Diego county line.

Orange County has some of the area's premier beaches and away-from-the-crowds hiking. Tidal basins, ecological preserves, undeveloped coastal canyons, and long beach strands follow the coastline along migratory routes for birds and gray whales. Among the county's highlights are beautiful Corona Del Mar (Hike 52) and undeveloped Crystal Cove State Park (Hikes 54—56).

San Diego County

Hikes 67—100 are located in San Diego County. The county's coastline has a diverse landscape composed of long stretches of sand and cobblestone beaches backed by steep, eroding sandstone bluffs. Long beach strands are interspersed with several major wetlands, large rivers, bays, estuaries, tidepools, and raised marine terraces.

One of the premier coastal preserves in the California state park system and one of the best hiking destinations in San Diego County is Torrey Pines State Reserve (Hikes 77—81). The park's magnificent features include pristine beaches, precipitous cliffs, oceanfront headlands with narrow ridges, sculpted gorges (cover photo), a 350-foot marine terrace, and wind-sculpted Torrey pines (the rarest pine in America).

San Diego County's many coastal highlights include the La Jolla Peninsula (Hikes 85—86), Mission Bay (Hikes 88—90), Point Loma and the Coronado Peninsula (Hikes 96—98), numerous wetland wildlife habitats, remote beaches accessed from cliffside stairways, and many outdoor recreational opportunities.

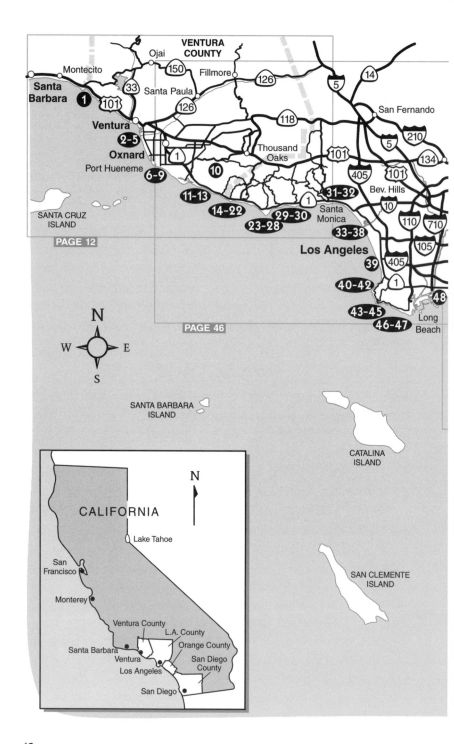

VENTURA COUNTY

Ojai
Montecito
Santa Barbara
Fillmore
Santa Paula
Ventura
Oxnard
Port Hueneme
San Fernando
Thousand Oaks
Santa Monica
Bev. Hills
Los Angeles
Long Beach

2-5
6-9
10
11-13
14-22
23-28
29-30
31-32
33-38
39
40-42
43-45
46-47
48

SANTA CRUZ ISLAND

PAGE 12

PAGE 46

N
W · E
S

SANTA BARBARA ISLAND

CATALINA ISLAND

SAN CLEMENTE ISLAND

N

CALIFORNIA

Lake Tahoe

San Francisco

Monterey

Ventura County
L.A. County
Santa Barbara
Ventura
Orange County
Los Angeles
San Diego County
San Diego

MAP OF THE HIKES
VENTURA • LOS ANGELES • ORANGE and SAN DIEGO COUNTIES

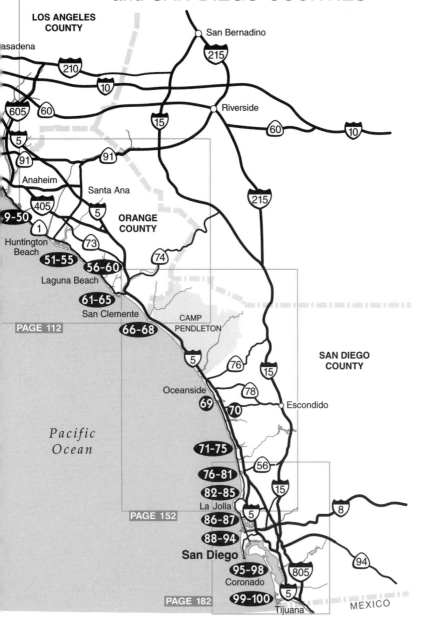

LOS ANGELES COUNTY

asadena

San Bernadino

215

210

10

605 60

Riverside

15

60

10

5

91

91

Anaheim

Santa Ana

215

405

ORANGE COUNTY

9-50

1

5

Huntington Beach

73

51-55

56-60

74

Laguna Beach

61-65

San Clemente

PAGE 112

66-68

CAMP PENDLETON

5

SAN DIEGO COUNTY

76

15

Oceanside

78

69

70

Escondido

Pacific Ocean

71-75

76-81

56

82-85

15

La Jolla

PAGE 152

86-87

5

88-94

San Diego

95-98

805

94

Coronado

PAGE 182

99-100

5

Tijuana

MEXICO

8

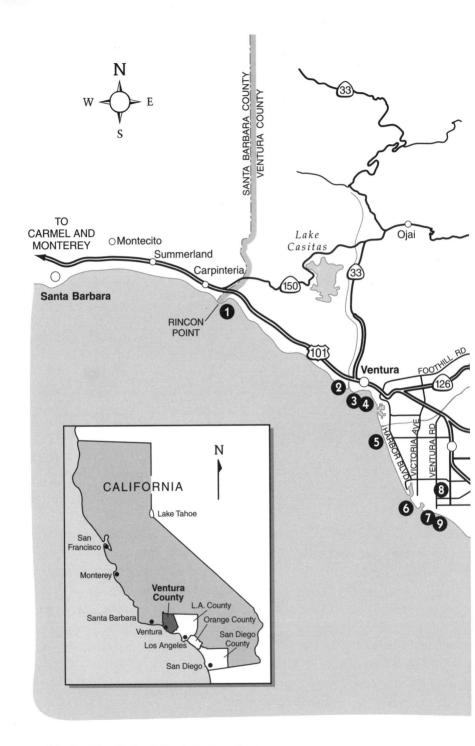

N
W ◎ E
S

TO CARMEL AND MONTEREY

◎ Montecito

Summerland

Carpinteria

Santa Barbara

RINCON POINT

1

Lake Casitas

Ojai

SANTA BARBARA COUNTY
VENTURA COUNTY

33

33

150

101

Ventura

FOOTHILL RD

126

2

3 4

5

HARBOR BLVD

VICTORIA AVE

VENTURA RD

8

6

7 9

N

CALIFORNIA

◎ Lake Tahoe

San Francisco

Monterey

Ventura County

L.A. County

Orange County

Santa Barbara

Ventura

San Diego County

Los Angeles

San Diego

HIKES 1–16
VENTURA COUNTY

Hike 1
Rincon Point and Rincon Beach Park

Hiking distance: 2 miles round trip
Hiking time: 1 hour
Elevation gain: 100 feet
Maps: U.S.G.S. White Ledge Peak
The Thomas Guide—Santa Barbara and Vicinity

Summary of hike: Rincon Point is a popular surfing spot with tidepools and a small bay. Rincon Beach Park is on the west side of the point. The park sits on the steep, forested bluff with eucalyptus trees and Monterey pines. There is a large picnic area, great views of the coastline, and a stairway to the 1,200 feet of beach frontage.

Driving directions: From Ventura, drive northbound on Highway 101 to the Ventura—Santa Barbara county line, and take the Bates Road exit. Turn left and cross Highway 101 one block to the parking lots. Park in the lots on either side of Bates Road.

From Santa Barbara, drive southbound on Highway 101. Continue 3 miles past Carpinteria, and take the Bates Road exit to the stop sign. Turn right, and park in the lots on either side of Bates Road.

Hiking directions: Begin from the Rincon Park parking lot on the right (west). From the edge of the cliffs, a long staircase and a paved service road both lead down the cliff face, providing access to the sandy shoreline and tidepools. Walk north along the beach, strolling past a series of tidepools along the base of the sandstone cliffs. After beachcombing, return to the parking lot. From the west end of the parking lot, a well-defined trail heads west past the metal gate. The path is a wide shelf cut on the steep cliffs high above the ocean. At 0.3 miles, the trail reaches the railroad tracks. The path parallels the railroad right-of-way west to Carpinteria. Choose your own turnaround spot.

From the Rincon Point parking lot on the east, take the wide beach access path. Descend through a shady, forested grove to the beach. Bear right on the rocky path to a small bay near the tree-lined point. This is an excellent area to explore the tidepools and watch the surfers. Return the way you came.

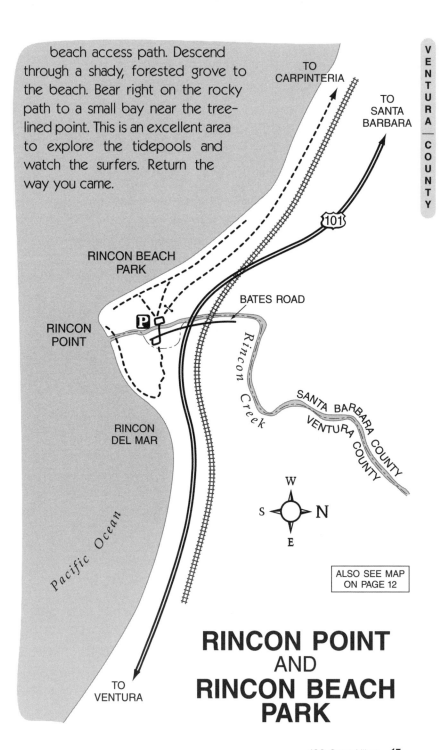

ALSO SEE MAP ON PAGE 12

RINCON POINT
AND
RINCON BEACH PARK

Hike 2
Ocean's Edge—River's Edge Loop
EMMA WOOD STATE BEACH · SEASIDE WILDERNESS PARK

Hiking distance: 2 mile loop
Hiking time: 1 hour
Elevation gain: Level
Maps: U.S.G.S. Ventura
      Emma Wood State Beach map

map
next page

Summary of hike: Emma Wood State Beach, located minutes from the city of Ventura, encompasses 152 acres near the mouth of the Ventura River. The state beach includes a campground, sand and cobblestone beaches, tidepools, sand dunes, a freshwater marsh, and thick riparian foliage. At the mouth of the river is an estuary where the freshwater from the river mixes with the salt water of the sea. Seaside Wilderness Park, adjacent to Emma Wood State Beach, is an undeveloped 22-acre park with a quarter mile of ocean frontage. The Ocean's Edge Trail begins in Emma Wood State Beach and follows the coastline past tidepools into the estuary and surrounding wetlands of Seaside Wilderness Park. The loop hike returns along the Ventura River on the River's Edge Trail.

Driving directions: Driving northbound on Highway 101 (Ventura Freeway) in Ventura, take the California Street exit. Drive a few blocks north to Main Street. Turn left and drive 1.2 miles through downtown Ventura to the Emma Wood State Beach entrance, just before reaching the northbound Highway 101 on-ramp. Turn left and drive 0.4 miles to the far end of the parking lot. A parking fee is required.

Driving southbound on Highway 101 (Ventura Freeway), take the Main Street/Ventura exit. At the end of the off-ramp, turn right and quickly turn right again into the posted Emma Wood State Beach.

Hiking directions: Take the paved walking path towards the railroad tracks and ocean. Cross through a tunnel under the tracks. Follow the natural path through the chaparral to the rocky oceanfront. Bear left on the Ocean's Edge Trail and stroll the coastline south. Cross a sandy stretch by the Second Mouth estuary, a former outlet of the Ventura River. Walk past the estuary and climb the low dunes to a network of connecting trails in Seaside Wilderness Park at the Ventura River. Bear left on the River's Edge Trail through riparian vegetation and groves of Monterey pines and palms. Parallel the north banks of the river in the Lower Ventura River Estuary. Cross over the railroad tracks, heading upstream to a bench overlooking a bend in the river. Curve away from the river on the wide path, weaving through a tunnel of trees. Cross the grassy picnic area, completing the loop at the parking lot.

Hike 3
San Buenaventura State Beach to the Ventura River Estuary

Hiking distance: 4 miles round trip
Hiking time: 2 hours
Elevation gain: Level
Maps: U.S.G.S. Ventura

map next page

Summary of hike: San Buenaventura State Beach is an oceanfront park extending two miles along Pierpont Bay. This hike begins at the park headquarters and follows the coastline west on a paved walking and biking path. The trail passes through Promenade Park (a grassy park at the edge of the beach), Surfers Point at Seaside Park (a popular surfing spot at the south end of Figueroa Street), and Ventura County Fairgrounds Beach (a rock and cobble beach). The hike ends at a wetland estuary where the Ventura River joins the ocean.

Driving directions: From Highway 101 (Ventura Freeway) in Ventura, exit on Seaward Avenue and head west to Harbor Boulevard. Turn right and drive 0.4 miles to San Pedro Street. Turn left and go 0.2 miles to the San Buenaventura State Beach parking lot on the right. A parking fee is required.

Hiking directions: Walk towards the ocean and the sand dunes. Take the paved walking and biking path to the right, heading northbound parallel to the dunes. At a half mile, the path closely parallels Harbor Boulevard. Cross a bridge over a lagoon formed by the San Jon Barranca drainage, reaching the Ventura Pier at just over a mile. For a short detour, walk up the steps and stroll 1,700 feet out to sea on the wooden pier. Continue west of the pier through landscaped Promenade Park, fronted by a wide, sandy beach. The sand soon gives way to the rocky shoreline at Surfers Point at Seaside Park and Ventura County Fairgrounds Beach, lined with palms. At the west end of the pathway, the trail turns inland along the Ventura River and estuary. Across the river is Seaside Wilderness Park and Emma Wood State Beach (Hike 2). This is our turnaround point.

To extend the hike, the Ventura River Trail crosses under Highway 101 and jogs through Ventura to a paved path. The trail continues to Foster Park off of Highway 33, where it becomes the Ojai Valley Trail. It continues 9.5 miles uphill on the old Southern Pacific Railroad to Libbey Park in downtown Ojai.

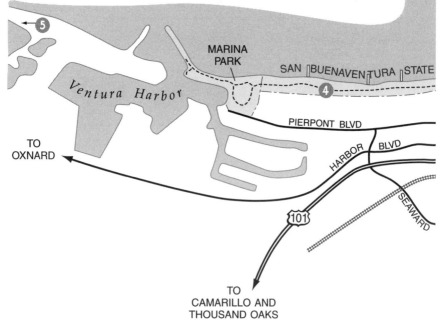

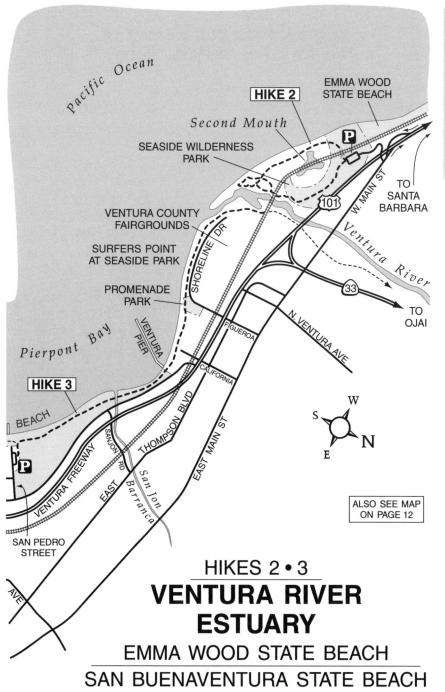

Pacific Ocean

HIKE 2

EMMA WOOD
STATE BEACH

Second Mouth

SEASIDE WILDERNESS
PARK

P

VENTURA COUNTY
FAIRGROUNDS

SHORELINE DR

101

W. MAIN ST

TO
SANTA
BARBARA

SURFERS POINT
AT SEASIDE PARK

Ventura River

PROMENADE
PARK

33

TO
OJAI

FIGUEROA

N. VENTURA AVE

VENTURA PIER

Pierpont Bay

CALIFORNIA

HIKE 3

BEACH

W

S

N

E

P

VENTURA FREEWAY

SANJON RD

THOMPSON BLVD

EAST

San Jon Barranca

EAST MAIN ST

ALSO SEE MAP
ON PAGE 12

SAN PEDRO
STREET

AVE

HIKES 2 • 3
VENTURA RIVER
ESTUARY
EMMA WOOD STATE BEACH
SAN BUENAVENTURA STATE BEACH

Hike 4
San Buenaventura State Beach to
Marina Park and Ventura Harbor

Hiking distance: 2.4 miles round trip
Hiking time: 1.5 hours
Elevation gain: Level
Maps: U.S.G.S. Ventura and Oxnard

Summary of hike: San Buenaventura State Beach extends for two miles along the Ventura coastline along a low dune ridge. Nestled in the southern portion of the state park is Marina Park, a palm-studded oceanfront park on the north peninsula of Ventura Harbor. The well-developed harbor was carved out of the dunes and has two separate marinas. The grassland park has sandy beaches, seagulls, playground equipment, and benches fronting the harbor. It is a great spot for observing boats coming in and out of the harbor.

Driving directions: From Highway 101 (Ventura Freeway) in Ventura, exit on Seaward Avenue and head west to Harbor Boulevard. Turn right and drive 0.4 miles to San Pedro Street. Turn left and go 0.2 miles to the San Buenaventura State Beach parking lot on the right. A parking fee is required.

Hiking directions: From the parking lot entrance, take the paved path 50 yards towards the beach. The paved path curves right (north)—Hike 3. Instead, take the sandy footpath towards the low dunes. Climb over the dunes to the shoreline by the rock breakwater. Follow the shoreline south, parallel to the beachfront homes behind the dunes. Pass a series of four rock groins that extend offshore to protect the beach from erosion. Continue along the shore, beyond the homes, into Marina Park. A paved path heads south across the peninsula to the Ventura Harbor Channel by sitting benches and a lone cypress. The trail ends at the harbor jetty. Return along the same route.

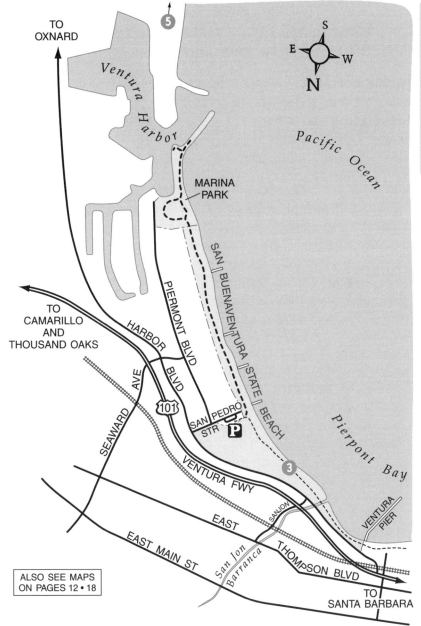

TO OXNARD

TO CAMARILLO AND THOUSAND OAKS

Ventura Harbor

Pacific Ocean

MARINA PARK

SAN BUENAVENTURA STATE BEACH

PIERMONT BLVD

HARBOR BLVD

SEAWARD AVE

101

SAN PEDRO STR

P

VENTURA FWY

EAST

EAST MAIN ST

San Jon Barranca

SAN JON

THOMPSON BLVD

Pierpont Bay

VENTURA PIER

TO SANTA BARBARA

ALSO SEE MAPS
ON PAGES 12 • 18

SAN BUENAVENTURA S.B.
TO MARINA PARK and VENTURA HARBOR

Hike 5
Santa Clara Estuary Natural Preserve
McGRATH STATE BEACH

Hiking distance: 0.7 mile loop to 4 miles round trip
Hiking time: 45 minutes—2 hours
Elevation gain: Level
Maps: U.S.G.S. Oxnard
McGrath State Beach map

Summary of hike: McGrath State Beach is located on the west end of Oxnard just south of Ventura. Rolling sand dunes, stabilized with vegetation, line the two-mile long coastline of this 295-acre park. The northern 160 acres comprise the Santa Clara Estuary Natural Preserve, where fresh water from the Santa Clara River mixes with the ocean's salt water. The Santa Clara Nature Trail follows the south banks of the river through the estuary and wildlife refuge, crossing low dunes to the ocean. McGrath Lake, a small freshwater lake at the southern end of McGrath State Beach, attracts hundreds of bird species.

Driving directions: From Highway 101 (Ventura Freeway) in Ventura, take the Victoria Avenue exit, and drive 0.6 miles south to Olivas Park Drive. Turn right and drive 2.4 miles to Harbor Boulevard. Turn left and continue 1.1 miles to the posted McGrath State Beach entrance at 2211 Harbor Boulevard. Turn right and go 0.2 miles to the trailhead parking lot, just beyond the entrance station. A parking fee is required.

Hiking directions: Walk to the far (north) end of the parking lot and curve right. Cross a wooden footbridge and enter a riparian habitat of sandbar willow thickets, cottonwoods, coastal scrub, and freshwater marsh plants. A raised boardwalk winds through the fragile wetlands to the banks of the Santa Clara River. Return 30 yards and continue on the path downstream to a levee. A path to the left returns to the parking area for a half-mile loop. Continue along the river and climb over the sand dunes to the mouth of the river at the ocean. This is a good turnaround spot for a shorter walk.

To extend the hike, follow the sandy coastline one mile south to the north end of McGrath Lake, peacefully hidden in the dunes. To spot it, walk to the top reaches of the beach, and drop down to the lake. Beyond the lake's south shore, the sandy coastline continues along Mandalay County Beach.

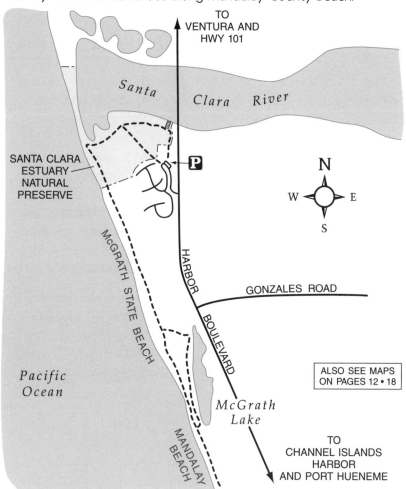

TO VENTURA AND HWY 101

Santa *Clara* *River*

SANTA CLARA ESTUARY NATURAL PRESERVE

P

N
W · E
S

GONZALES ROAD

HARBOR

BOULEVARD

McGRATH STATE BEACH

Pacific Ocean

ALSO SEE MAPS ON PAGES 12 • 18

McGrath Lake

MANDALAY BEACH

TO CHANNEL ISLANDS HARBOR AND PORT HUENEME

SANTA CLARA ESTUARY NATURAL PRESERVE
McGRATH STATE BEACH

Hike 6
Silver Strand Beach to La Janelle Park

Hiking distance: 2.5 miles round trip
Hiking time: 1.5 hours
Elevation gain: Level
Maps: U.S.G.S. Oxnard

Summary of hike: Silver Strand Beach is a level, white sand beach that fronts a small pocket community in Oxnard. The beach stretches one mile from the mouth of Channel Islands Harbor to Point Hueneme, at the mouth of Port Hueneme Harbor. La Janelle Park sits on Point Hueneme at the south end of the sandy beach. The park borders the Port Hueneme Naval Construction Battalion Center, which nearly surrounds Port Hueneme Harbor. This hike strolls along the oceanfront from Channel Islands Harbor to La Janelle Park.

In April, 1970, the S.S. La Jenelle, a 12,000-ton pleasure ship, ran aground in a storm. The wreck, just offshore of Point Hueneme, was filled with rocks and converted into a fishing jetty. The park and offshore area is now a popular fishing and surfing spot.

Driving directions: From Highway 101 (Ventura Freeway) in Ventura, take the Victoria Avenue exit. Drive 6.6 miles south to the end of Victoria Avenue at the junction with San Nicholas Avenue. Park in the lot on the right, just before reaching San Nicholas Avenue.

Hiking directions: Follow the paved Channel Islands Harbor walking path southwest on the elevated rock jetty. Pass Ocean Drive to the sandy beachfront by the lifeguard station. At the end of the path are benches for watching the surf and boats entering and exiting the harbor. Head south, strolling along the wide sandy beach, fronted by homes. At the south end of the beach is Point Hueneme, jutting out to sea with two rock jetties. (The west jetty is built upon the S.S. La Jenelle ruins.) A fence separates La Janelle Park from the military center. Return along the same route or follow the fenceline on the unpaved road to Ocean Drive. Bear left on Ocean Drive, returning to the Channel Islands Harbor.

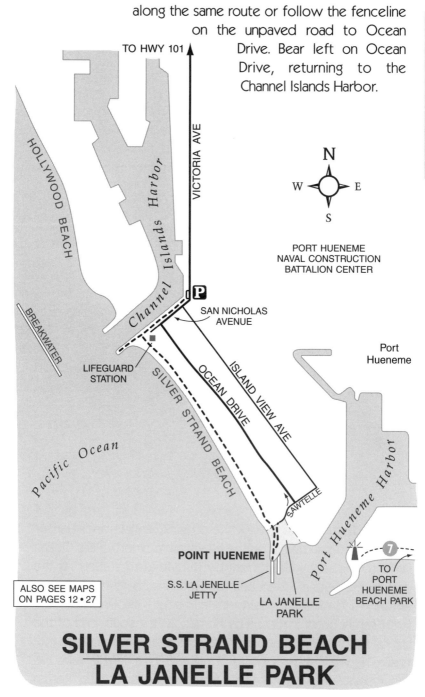

N
W E
S

TO HWY 101

VICTORIA AVE

Hollywood Beach

Channel Islands Harbor

BREAKWATER

P

SAN NICHOLAS AVENUE

LIFEGUARD STATION

SILVER STRAND BEACH

OCEAN DRIVE

ISLAND VIEW AVE

PORT HUENEME NAVAL CONSTRUCTION BATTALION CENTER

Port Hueneme

Port Hueneme Harbor

Pacific Ocean

SAWTELLE

POINT HUENEME

S.S. LA JENELLE JETTY

LA JANELLE PARK

7

TO PORT HUENEME BEACH PARK

ALSO SEE MAPS ON PAGES 12 • 27

SILVER STRAND BEACH
LA JANELLE PARK

Hike 7
Port Hueneme Beach Park

Hiking distance: 2.5 miles round trip
Hiking time: 1.5 hours
Elevation gain: Level
Maps: U.S.G.S. Oxnard

Summary of hike: Port Hueneme Beach Park is a landscaped and well-maintained park to the southeast of the 1,600-acre Port Hueneme Naval Construction Battalion Center. The 50-acre park has a wide sandy beach and a wooden, T-shaped recreational pier that extends 1,240 feet out to sea. From the pier are great views of the Ventura County coastline, the Channel Islands, and the Santa Monica Mountains at Point Mugu. A path runs along the edge of the beach, ending at the harbor entrance of the naval complex.

Driving directions: Heading northbound on Highway 101 (Ventura Freeway) in Oxnard, take the Ventura Road exit, and drive 7 miles south to Surfside Drive at the beachfront. Turn left and drive 0.2 miles to the beach parking lot on the right. A parking fee is required.

Heading southbound on Highway 101 (Ventura Freeway) in Oxnard, take the Wagon Wheel Road exit, and turn right a half block to Ventura Road. Turn left and drive 7 miles south to Surfside Drive at the beachfront.

Hiking directions: Take the paved, palm-lined path curving south and looping by Bubbling Springs (Hike 8). Heading southeast away from the walkway is Ormand Beach (Hike 9), an undeveloped natural area with low rolling sand dunes and a wide sandy beach that extends 3 miles along the coast. Port Hueneme Beach Park lies west towards Port Hueneme Pier. Stroll out on the pier, and take in the sweeping vistas from offshore. Continue west from the pier, either beachcombing or following the walking path to the west end of Surfside Drive. Beyond the walkway, a wide gravel path follows the shoreline to the mouth of Port Hueneme Harbor, between the ocean-front jetty boulders and the shipping docks. At the harbor channel is the Port Hueneme Lighthouse, originally built in 1874 and rebuilt in 1941. Across the channel is Point Hueneme, Hike 6. Return by retracing your steps.

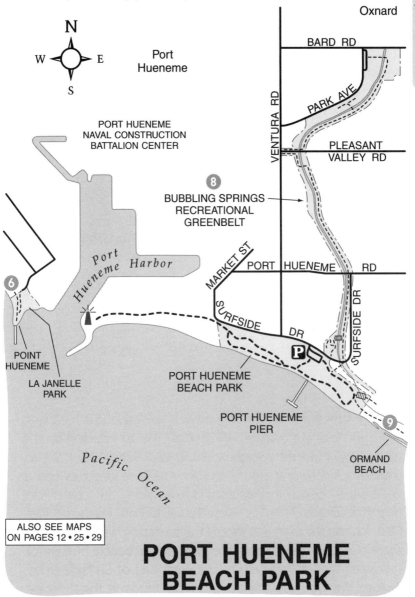

**PORT HUENEME
BEACH PARK**

Hike 8
Bubbling Springs Recreational Greenbelt

Hiking distance: 3.6 miles round trip
Hiking time: 2 hours
Elevation gain: Level
Maps: U.S.G.S. Oxnard
       The Thomas Guide—Ventura County

Summary of hike: Bubbling Springs Park is a long, narrow greenbelt extending from Port Hueneme's inner residential area to the ocean at Port Hueneme Beach Park. A 1.5-mile hiking and biking path winds through the landscaped recreational corridor alongside tranquil Bubbling Springs, a tree-shaded drainage channel.

Driving directions: From Highway 101 (Ventura Freeway) in Oxnard, take the Ventura Road exit, and drive 6 miles south to Bard Road. Turn left and drive 0.3 miles to Bubbling Springs Park. Turn right on Park Avenue and park in the spaces on the left.

Heading southbound on Highway 101 (Ventura Freeway) in Oxnard, take the Wagon Wheel Road exit, and turn right a half block to Ventura Road. Turn left and drive 6 miles south to Bard Road. Turn left and drive 0.3 miles to Bubbling Springs Park. Turn right on Park Avenue and park in the spaces on the left.

Hiking directions: Cross the grassy park by the ball fields to the paved hiking and biking path on the east edge of the greenbelt. Take the path to the right, and head south alongside Bubbling Springs, lined with eucalyptus trees. At 0.3 miles is a bridge crossing over the stream to an open parkland. The path stays on the east side of the waterway, passing the community center to Pleasant Valley Road at 0.6 miles. Cross the intersection at Ventura Road, and continue on the signed walking path. Curve left, crossing a bridge over the creek, and follow the tree-lined watercourse downstream, reaching Port Hueneme Road at 1.1 miles. Cross the boulevard and continue south, parallel to the creek and Surfside Drive. Another bridge crosses the creek to an expansive grassy section of Bubbling Springs Linear Park and its baseball fields. The streamside trail meanders through palm tree groves to Surfside Drive. Cross the road to Port Hueneme Beach Park, where the trail ends. To extend the hike along the coastline, continue with Hikes 7 and 9.

ALSO SEE MAPS
ON PAGES 12 • 27 • 31

BUBBLING SPRINGS
RECREATIONAL GREENBELT

Hike 9
Ormand Beach

Hiking distance: 4 miles round trip
Hiking time: 2 hours
Elevation gain: Level
Maps: U.S.G.S. Oxnard and Point Mugu

Summary of hike: Ormand Beach is a 865-acre undeveloped beach in Oxnard that is off the beaten track. The beach stretches nearly 5 miles, from Port Hueneme Beach Park to Point Mugu Naval Air Station. It is backed by acres of farmland and has an extensive dune structure. The beach also includes a salt marsh wetland preserve, mudflats, and a freshwater lagoon fed by ground water and agricultural runoff. The preserve is on the Pacific Flyway, a 2,000-mile migratory route providing habitat for birds between Alaska and Latin America. The wetlands are also a nesting ground for the endangered western snowy plover, California least tern, and the California brown pelican. The coastal walk explores the dunes and coastal wetlands, following water channels parallel to the ocean.

Driving directions: Same as Hike 7.

Hiking directions: From the far south end of the parking lot, take the paved path to a wooden bridge crossing Bubbling Springs. Just before the bridge, curve right on the wide gravel path. Follow the bank of the water channel to the lagoon. Head south on the sandy dune/channel between the lagoon and the ocean. Stroll through the wetland bird sanctuary, parallel to the water channel, to another bridge. The bridge crosses over the water channel and heads inland to Perkins Road and a parking lot at the wastewater treatment plant. (This is another access to Ormand Beach, located 0.6 miles south from Hueneme Road.) Continue south on the isolated coastal stretch through the wetlands to the fenced boundary of Point Mugu Naval Air Station. An asphalt path parallels the naval station and crosses a bridge to Arnold Road, the southern beach access parking lot at the end of the road, 1.7 miles south of Hueneme Road. Return along the same route.

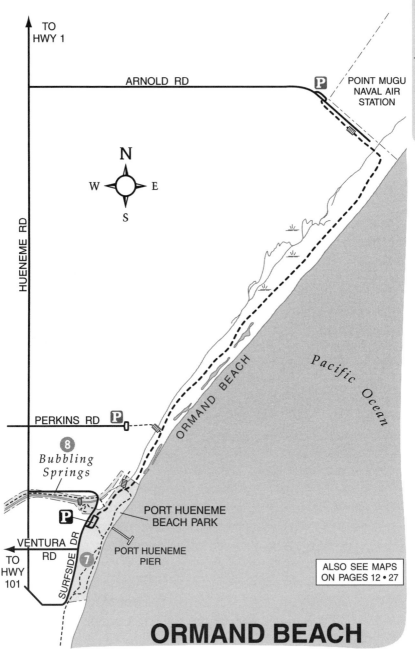

TO
HWY 1

ARNOLD RD

POINT MUGU
NAVAL AIR
STATION

N
W ◆ E
S

HUENEME RD

Pacific Ocean

ORMAND BEACH

PERKINS RD

⑧
*Bubbling
Springs*

PORT HUENEME
BEACH PARK

VENTURA
RD
TO
HWY
101

SURFSIDE DR

⑦

PORT HUENEME
PIER

ALSO SEE MAPS
ON PAGES 12 • 27

ORMAND BEACH

Hike 10
Big Sycamore Canyon Trail
POINT MUGU STATE PARK

Hiking distance: 8.4 miles one way (car shuttle)
Hiking time: 3 hours
Elevation loss: 900 feet
Maps: U.S.G.S. Newbury Park, Camarillo, and Point Mugu
      Santa Monica Mountains West Trail Map
      N.P.S. Rancho Sierra Vista/Satwiwa map

Summary of hike: The Big Sycamore Canyon Trail is a one-way mountains-to the-sea journey. The trail, an unpaved service road, connects Newbury Park with the Sycamore Canyon Campground at the Pacific Ocean. The hike parallels Big Sycamore Creek through the heart of Point Mugu State Park in a deep, wooded canyon under towering sycamores and oaks.

Driving directions: For the shuttle car, follow the driving directions to Hike 13 and leave the car in the parking lot, where this hike ends.

    To the trailhead: From the shuttle car parking lot, drive 5.8 miles northbound on the Pacific Coast Highway (Highway 1) to Las Posas Road. Take Las Posas Road 2.9 miles north to Hueneme Road—turn right. Continue one mile to West Potrero Road and turn right. Drive 5.4 miles to Via Goleta and turn right (En route, West Potrero Road becomes Lynn Road). Drive 0.7 miles on Via Goleta to the parking lot at the end of the road.

Hiking directions: Take the posted trail past the restrooms a quarter mile to the service road at the Satwiwa Native American Indian Cultural Center. Bear right on the road, entering Point Mugu State Park, to a junction with the Boney Mountain Trail on the left. Begin the winding descent on the paved road to the canyon floor. The trail crosses a wooden bridge over the creek to the Hidden Pond Trail junction on the right. This is an excellent single track alternative trail that rejoins the Big Sycamore Canyon Trail 1.7 miles down canyon. On the alternative trail, there is a split at 2.2 miles. Take the left fork to the Sycamore Camping and Picnic Area. At 3 miles is a signed "beach" path on the right. This is where the alternative trail rejoins the service road. Just past the junction is the Danielson Ranch. Past the ranch, the trail is unpaved. Continue south down the forested canyon, past the Backbone Trail and the Overlook Trail (Hike 13) to the gate. From the gate, a paved road leads back to the shuttle car.

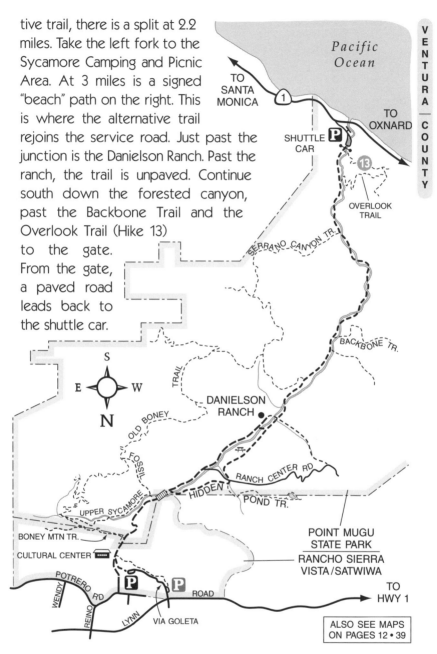

BIG SYCAMORE CANYON
POINT MUGU STATE PARK

Hike 11
Chumash Trail—Mugu Peak Loop
POINT MUGU STATE PARK

Hiking distance: 4.5 mile loop
Hiking time: 2.5 hours
Elevation gain: 1,100 feet
Maps: U.S.G.S. Point Mugu
 Santa Monica Mountains West Trail Map

map next page

Summary of hike: La Jolla Valley Natural Preserve is an expansive high-mountain valley at the far western end of the Santa Monica Mountains. The oak-studded grassland rests 800 feet above the ocean at the foot of Mugu Peak. The high ridges of Laguna Peak, La Jolla Peak, and the serrated Boney Mountain ridgeline surround the rolling meadow. La Jolla Valley can be accessed from La Jolla Canyon (Hike 12), Big Sycamore Canyon (Hike 10), and the Chumash Trail (this hike), the steepest and most direct route. For centuries, this trail was a Chumash Indian route connecting their coastal village at Mugu Lagoon with La Jolla Valley. This hike steeply ascends the coastal slope on the west flank of Mugu Peak. The elevated Mugu Peak Trail circles the mountain slope below the double peak, with sweeping ocean and mountain vistas.

Driving directions: From Santa Monica, drive 35 miles northbound on the Pacific Coast Highway (Highway 1) to the large parking pullout on the right, across from the Navy Rifle Range and Mugu Lagoon. (The trailhead parking area is 16.8 miles past Kanan Dume Road in Malibu and 3.5 miles west of the well-marked Sycamore Canyon.)

Heading southbound on the Pacific Coast Highway (Highway 1) from Las Posas Road in southeast Oxnard, drive 2.3 miles to the parking area on the left by the posted trailhead.

Hiking directions: Begin climbing up the chaparral and cactus covered hillside, gaining elevation with every step. At a half mile, the trail temporarily levels out on a plateau with sweeping coastal views, including the Channel Islands. The steadily ascending trail gains 900 feet in 0.7 miles to a T-junction on a saddle. Begin the loop to the left, crossing over the saddle into the vast La Jolla Valley. The valley is surrounded by rounded mountain peaks, the jagged Boney Mountain ridge, and the surrealistic Navy radar towers by Laguna Peak. Cross the open expanse to a posted junction with the La Jolla Valley Loop Trail at 1.2 miles. Take the right fork and head southeast across the meadow on a slight downward slope. Drop into an oak woodland and cross a stream. Parallel the stream through a small draw to a another junction. Take the right fork 100 yards to a path on the right by an old circular metal tank. Bear right on the Mugu Peak Trail and cross the creek. Traverse the hillside to the west edge of La Jolla Canyon. Follow the ridge south on the oceanfront cliffs. Wind along the south flank of Mugu Peak, following the contours of the mountain to a trail split on a saddle between the mountain's double peaks. The right fork ascends the rounded grassy summit. Veer left, hiking along the steep hillside to the west side of the peak. Cross another saddle and complete the loop. Return down the mountain to the trailhead.

Hike 12
La Jolla Valley Loop from La Jolla Canyon
POINT MUGU STATE PARK

Hiking distance: 6 miles round trip
Hiking time: 3 hours
Elevation gain: 750 feet
Maps: U.S.G.S. Point Mugu
        Santa Monica Mountains West Trail Map

map
next page

Summary of hike: La Jolla Canyon is a narrow, steep gorge with a perennial stream and a 15-foot waterfall. The canyon leads up to La Jolla Valley Natural Preserve at an 800-foot elevation, a broad valley with rolling grasslands at the west end of the Santa Monica Mountains. Mugu Peak, La Jolla Peak, and Laguna Peak surround the oak-dotted meadow. This hike climbs through the rock-walled canyon and loops around the meadow to a coastal overlook and a pond with a picnic area.

Driving directions: From Santa Monica, drive 33 miles northbound on the Pacific Coast Highway (Highway 1) to the posted La Jolla Canyon entrance on the right. (The trailhead entrance is 15 miles past Kanan Dume Road in Malibu and 1.6 miles west of the well-marked Sycamore Canyon.)

Heading southbound on the Pacific Coast Highway (Highway 1) from Las Posas Road in southeast Oxnard, drive 4.2 miles to the entrance on the left.

Hiking directions: From the north end of the parking lot, at the Ray Miller Trailhead, take the La Jolla Canyon Trail north. Follow the wide path up the canyon, crossing the stream several times. The third crossing is just below a beautiful 15-foot waterfall and a pool surrounded by large boulders. Natural rock steps lead up to the top of the falls. Continue along the east side of the canyon, passing large sandstone rocks and caves. At a gorge, the trail sharply doubles back to the right, leading up the side of the canyon. At 1.2 miles, take the left fork towards Mugu Peak. Cross the stream and head southwest to a ridge above La Jolla Canyon and the ocean. The trail levels out and passes two trail junctions. Stay to the right both times, heading north across the rolling grassland. At 2.7 miles the trail joins the wide La Jolla Valley Loop Trail—head to the right. As you near the mountains of La Jolla Canyon, take the first cutoff trail to the right, leading past the pond and rejoining the La Jolla Canyon Trail. Head to the right, and go two miles down canyon, returning to the trailhead.

TO OXNARD

Mugu Lagoon

HIKES 11•12
LA JOLLA VALLEY
MUGU PEAK
POINT MUGU STATE PARK

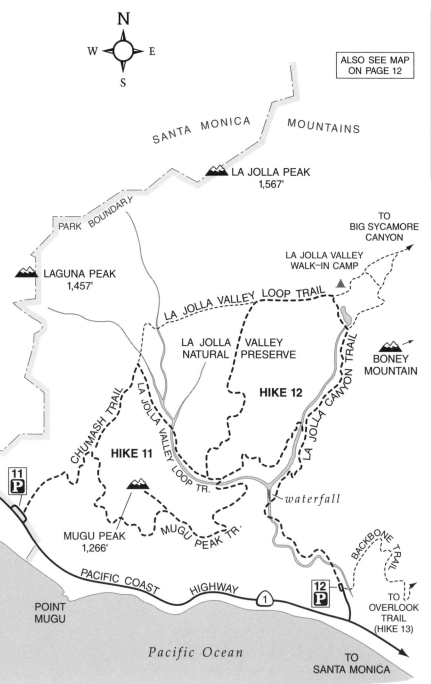

N

W ← → E

S

ALSO SEE MAP
ON PAGE 12

SANTA MONICA MOUNTAINS

LA JOLLA PEAK
1,567'

PARK BOUNDARY

TO
BIG SYCAMORE
CANYON

LA JOLLA VALLEY
WALK-IN CAMP

LAGUNA PEAK
1,457'

LA JOLLA VALLEY LOOP TRAIL

LA JOLLA
NATURAL PRESERVE
VALLEY

BONEY
MOUNTAIN

CHUMASH TRAIL

LA JOLLA CANYON TRAIL

HIKE 12

LA JOLLA VALLEY LOOP TR.

HIKE 11

MUGU PEAK
1,266'

MUGU PEAK TR.

waterfall

BACKBONE TRAIL

11
P

12
P

PACIFIC COAST HIGHWAY

1

TO
OVERLOOK
TRAIL
(HIKE 13)

POINT
MUGU

Pacific Ocean

TO
SANTA MONICA

Hike 13
Scenic and Overlook Trails Loop
POINT MUGU STATE PARK

Hiking distance: 2 mile loop
Hiking time: 1 hour
Elevation gain: 900 feet
Maps: U.S.G.S. Point Mugu
       Santa Monica Mountains West Trail Map

Summary of hike: The Scenic and Overlook Trails are located along the coastal frontage of Point Mugu State Park. The trail follows the ridge separating Big Sycamore Canyon from La Jolla Canyon. This short but beautiful hike climbs up the chaparral-covered ridge to several panoramic overlooks of the Pacific Ocean.

Driving directions: From Santa Monica, drive 31 miles northbound on the Pacific Coast Highway (Highway 1) to the posted Point Mugu State Park entrance on the right. (The trailhead entrance is 13.3 miles past Kanan Dume Road in Malibu and 5.3 miles west of the well-marked Leo Carrillo State Beach.) Turn right and park in the day-use pay parking lot 0.1 mile ahead on the left. (Parking is free in the pullouts along the PCH.)

Heading southbound on the Pacific Coast Highway (Highway 1) from Las Posas Road in southeast Oxnard, drive 5.8 miles to the Sycamore Canyon entrance on the left.

Hiking directions: From the parking area, walk up the road past the campground to the Big Sycamore Canyon trailhead gate. Continue up the unpaved road about 50 yards to the signed junction with the Scenic Trail. Take the trail to the left (west) across Big Sycamore Creek, and head up the wooden steps. The trail steadily gains elevation up an open, grassy hillside with good canyon views. At the saddle near the top of the hill is a trail split. The left fork leads a short distance to an ocean overlook. Continue up to several more viewpoints. Return back to the junction, and head north to a junction with the Overlook Trail. Take this service road downhill to the right, winding 0.9 miles back to the Big Sycamore Canyon floor. Near the bottom, a series of five gentle switchbacks lead to the junction. Take the canyon trail to the right, leading 0.4 miles back to the trailhead gate.

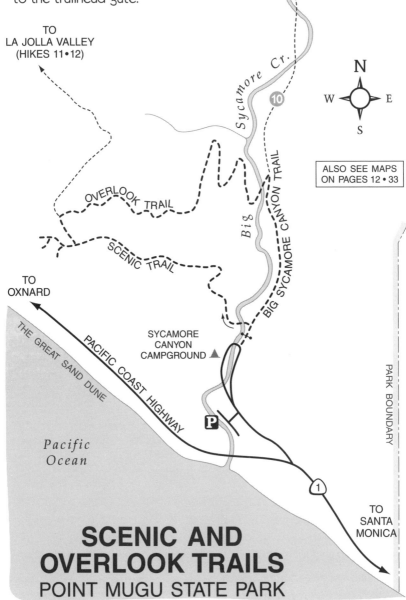

TO
LA JOLLA VALLEY
(HIKES 11•12)

Sycamore Cr.

10

N
W E
S

ALSO SEE MAPS
ON PAGES 12 • 33

OVERLOOK TRAIL

Big

BIG SYCAMORE CANYON TRAIL

SCENIC TRAIL

TO
OXNARD

THE GREAT SAND DUNE

PACIFIC COAST HIGHWAY

SYCAMORE
CANYON
CAMPGROUND ▲

PARK BOUNDARY

P

Pacific
Ocean

1

TO
SANTA
MONICA

**SCENIC AND
OVERLOOK TRAILS**
POINT MUGU STATE PARK

Hike 14
Grotto Trail
CIRCLE X RANCH

Hiking distance: 3.5 miles round trip
Hiking time: 2 hours
Elevation gain: 650 feet
Maps: U.S.G.S. Triunfo Pass
Santa Monica Mountains West Trail Map
N.P.S. Circle X Ranch Site

Summary of hike: The Grotto Trail is located in the 1,655-acre Circle X Ranch bordering Point Mugu State Park. Once a Boy Scout wilderness retreat, the Circle X Ranch is now a national park and recreation area. The Grotto, at the end of this trail, is a maze of large, volcanic boulders in a sheer, narrow gorge formed from landslides. The West Fork of the Arroyo Sequit flows through the caves and caverns of The Grotto, creating cascades and pools.

Driving directions: From the Pacific Coast Highway (Highway 1) in Santa Monica, drive 38 miles northbound to Yerba Buena Road and turn right. (Yerba Buena Road is 10.1 miles past Kanan Dume Road and 2 miles past Leo Carrillo State Beach.) Continue 5.3 miles up the winding road to the Circle X Ranger Station on the right. Park by the ranger station, or continue 0.2 miles downhill to the day-use parking area, just past the posted Grotto Trailhead.

From the Pacific Coast Highway (Highway 1) and Las Posas Road in southeast Oxnard, drive 9 miles southbound to Yerba Buena Road (3.3 miles past Big Sycamore Canyon) and follow the directions above.

Hiking directions: From the ranger station, walk 0.2 miles down the unpaved road to the posted Grotto trailhead, just before reaching the lower parking area. Continue downhill, crossing the West Fork of Arroyo Sequit. At 0.4 miles, the trail passes the Canyon View Trail (Hike 15) and recrosses the creek at a 30-foot waterfall. After crossing, curve left, traversing a grassy ridge. Descend to the canyon floor where the trail joins the Happy Hollow Campground Road at 1.2 miles. Follow the road to the left into a primitive campground and cross the creek, picking up the posted Grotto Trail again. Head downstream to a bridge that crosses the creek into the Happy Hollow Campground. Instead of crossing the bridge, continue straight ahead and cross the creek by a pumphouse. Follow the creek a few hundred feet to The Grotto.

After exploring The Grotto, return to the bridge that accesses the campground. Walk through the campground to the road and bear to the right. Follow the winding road, and rejoin the Grotto Trail on the left. Retrace your steps to the parking lot.

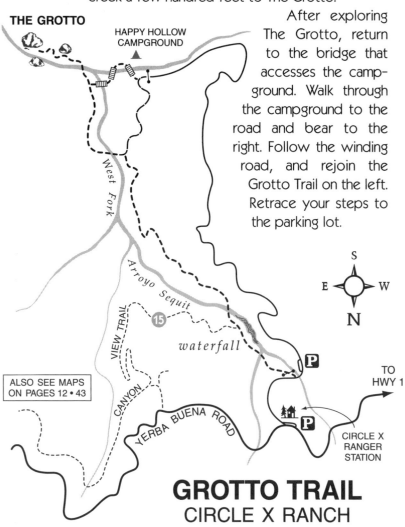

THE GROTTO

HAPPY HOLLOW CAMPGROUND

West Fork

Arroyo Sequit

15

VIEW TRAIL

waterfall

CANYON

YERBA BUENA ROAD

ALSO SEE MAPS ON PAGES 12 • 43

TO HWY 1

CIRCLE X RANGER STATION

GROTTO TRAIL
CIRCLE X RANCH

Hike 15
Canyon View—
Yerba Buena Road Loop
CIRCLE X RANCH

Hiking distance: 3.2 mile loop
Hiking time: 1.5 hours
Elevation gain: 500 feet
Maps: U.S.G.S. Triunfo Pass
Santa Monica Mountains West Trail Map
N.P.S. Circle X Ranch Site

Summary of hike: Circle X Ranch sits below Boney Mountain in the upper canyons of Arroyo Sequit. The Canyon View Trail traverses the brushy hillside of the deep, east-facing canyon. The panoramic views extend down the canyon to the Pacific Ocean. The northern views reach the jagged Boney Mountain ridge and the 3,111-foot Sandstone Peak, the highest peak in the Santa Monica Mountains. The trail connects the Grotto Trail (Hike 14) with the Backbone Trail (Hike 16).

Driving directions: Same as Hike 14.

Hiking directions: From the ranger station, walk 0.2 miles down the unpaved road to the posted Grotto Trailhead, just before reaching the lower parking area. Pass the trail gate and follow the dirt road past a picnic area to another trail sign. Take the footpath downhill and cross the West Fork Arroyo Creek. Parallel the east side of the creek to a signed junction. (Twenty yards to the right is a waterfall—Hike 14.) Bear left on the Canyon View Trail, and traverse the canyon wall, following the contours of the mountain. Climb two switchbacks to a junction. For a shorter 1.5-mile loop, take the Connector Trail 100 yards to the left, reaching Yerba Buena Road, and return 0.35 miles to the ranger station. For this longer hike, stay to the right and cross a rocky wash. Head up the hillside to a south view down canyon to the ocean and the Channel Islands and a north view of the Boney Mountain ridge. Continue to Yerba Buena Road, across from the Backbone Trail (Hike 16). Return to the left on Yerba Buena Road, and walk 1.1 miles back to the trailhead at the Circle X Ranger Station.

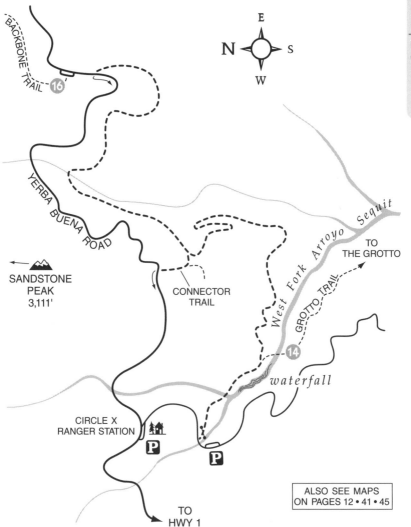

CANYON VIEW TRAIL– YERBA BUENA ROAD
CIRCLE X RANCH

Hike 16
Mishe Mokwa—Backbone Loop
Sandstone Peak
CIRCLE X RANCH

Hiking distance: 6 mile loop
Hiking time: 3 hours
Elevation gain: 1,100 feet
Maps: U.S.G.S. Triunfo Pass and Newbury Park
Santa Monica Mountains West Trail Map
N.P.S. Circle X Ranch Site

Summary of hike: The Mishe Mokwa Trail in Circle X Ranch follows Carlisle Canyon along Boney Mountain past weathered red volcanic formations. There are views of the sculpted caves and crevices of Echo Cliffs and a forested streamside picnic area by a huge, split boulder known as Split Rock. The return route on the Backbone Trail leads to Inspiration Point and Sandstone Peak, the highest point in the Santa Monica Mountains. Both points overlook the Pacific Ocean, the Channel Islands, and the surrounding mountains.

Driving directions: Follow directions for Hike 14 to the Circle X Ranger Station. From the ranger station, continue one mile to the Backbone Trailhead parking lot on the left.

Hiking directions: Take the Backbone Trail (a fire road) uphill to the north. At 0.3 miles, leave the road and take the signed Mishe Mokwa Connector Trail straight ahead. Continue 0.2 miles to a junction with the Mishe Mokwa Trail and take the left fork. The trail contours along Boney Mountain on the western edge of Carlisle Canyon. At 1.4 miles, Balanced Rock can be seen on the opposite side of the canyon. Descend into the canyon shaded by oaks, laurel, and sycamores to Split Rock and the picnic area. Take the trail across the stream, heading out of the canyon to another stream crossing by sculptured volcanic rocks. Parallel the stream to a signed junction. Take the left fork—the Backbone Trail—curving uphill towards Inspiration

Point. A short side path leads up to the overlook. Continue east on the Backbone Trail to another junction. This side trail switchbacks up to the 360-degree views at Sandstone Peak. From the junction, it is 0.8 miles downhill back to the Mishe Mokwa junction, completing the loop.

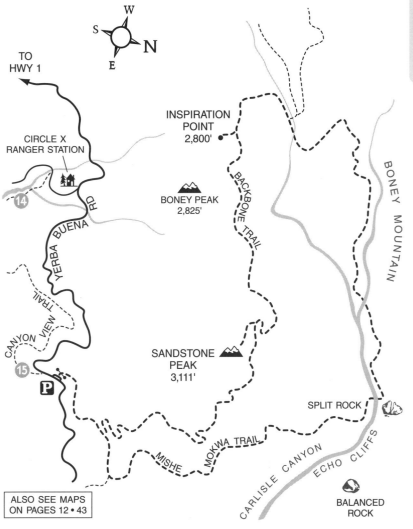

SANDSTONE PEAK LOOP
CIRCLE X RANCH

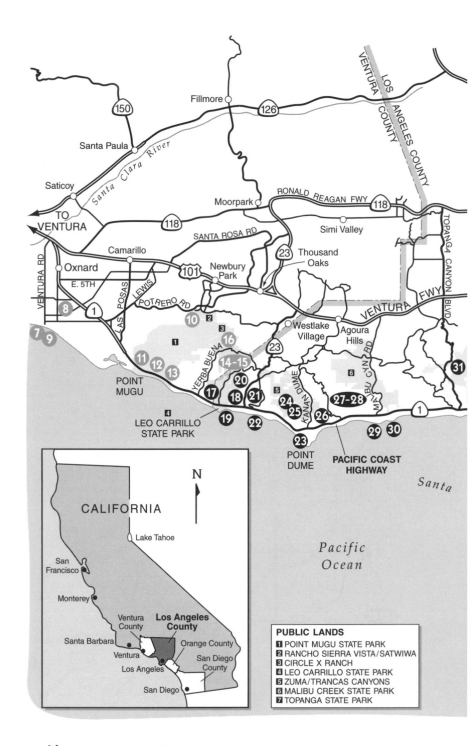

Fillmore

(150)

(126)

Santa Paula

Santa Clara River

Saticoy

TO VENTURA

Moorpark

RONALD REAGAN FWY

(118)

(118)

SANTA ROSA RD

Simi Valley

Camarillo

(23)

Thousand Oaks

Oxnard

(101)

Newbury Park

E. 5TH

LEWIS

POTRERO RD

Westlake Village

Agoura Hills

VENTURA

FWY

8

(1)

7 **9**

10

2

3

16

1

11 **12** **13**

YERBA BUENA

14-15

(23)

6

31

POINT MUGU

20

17

18 **21**

5

24

KANAN DUME

27-28

4

19

22

25

26

(1)

LEO CARRILLO STATE PARK

29 **30**

23

POINT DUME

PACIFIC COAST HIGHWAY

Santa

N

CALIFORNIA

Lake Tahoe

San Francisco

Monterey

Ventura County

Los Angeles County

Santa Barbara

Orange County

Ventura

San Diego County

Los Angeles

San Diego

Pacific Ocean

PUBLIC LANDS

1 POINT MUGU STATE PARK
2 RANCHO SIERRA VISTA/SATWIWA
3 CIRCLE X RANCH
4 LEO CARRILLO STATE PARK
5 ZUMA/TRANCAS CANYONS
6 MALIBU CREEK STATE PARK
7 TOPANGA STATE PARK

LOS ANGELES | COUNTY

N
W E
S

5
118
GOLDEN STATE
210
FOOTHILL FWY
5 FWY
405
170
134
2
110
HOLLYWOOD FWY
101
2 DOWNTOWN LOS ANGELES
210
SAN DIEGO
SAN BERNADINO 10 FWY
60 POMONA FWY
SANTA 10 MONICA FWY
605
Santa Monica
33–38
MARINA DEL REY
FWY
110
710
SANTA ANA FWY
L.A. CTY
ORANGE CTY
7
DETAIL PAGE 80
105
5
32
Monica Bay
1
39
91
LONG BEACH FWY
Los Angeles River
San Gabriel River
SAN GABRIEL
TO SAN DIEGO
40–42
PACIFIC COAST HWY
48
Seal Beach
405
PALOS VERDES PENINSULA
HAWTHORNE
43–44 45
PALOS VERDES DR
46–47
LOS ANGELES HARBOR
1
TO SAN DIEGO

Hike 17
Yellow Hill Trail
LEO CARRILLO STATE BEACH

Hiking distance: 5 miles round trip
Hiking time: 2.5 hours
Elevation gain: 1,300 feet
Maps: U.S.G.S. Triunfo Pass
      Santa Monica Mountains West Trail Map
      Leo Carrillo State Beach map

Summary of hike: The Yellow Hill Trail is within Leo Carrillo State Beach, a 3,000-acre park at the western tip of Los Angeles County. The trail steadily climbs a fire road up Sequit Ridge in the backcountry hills. The trailhead begins on the west side of Mulholland Highway in Los Angeles County and follows the mountain ridge, leaving the west side of the state park into Ventura County. En route are outstanding ocean views, including the four Channel Islands.

Driving directions: Heading northbound on the Pacific Coast Highway (Highway 1) from Santa Monica, drive 14 miles past Malibu Canyon Road and 8 miles past Kanan Dume Road to Mulholland Highway. It is located 0.2 miles past the Leo Carrillo State Beach entrance. Turn right and go 100 yards to the gated fire road on the left. Park along the side of the road. Parking is also available in Leo Carrillo State Beach off PCH.

From the Pacific Coast Highway (Highway 1) and Las Posas Road in southeast Oxnard, drive 10.8 miles southbound on PCH to Mulholland Highway, just before the posted Leo Carrillo State Beach entrance. Proceed with the directions above.

Hiking directions: Walk around the trailhead gate, and follow the old dirt road, passing prickly pear cactus. Coastal views quickly open up, from Point Dume to Point Mugu and across the ocean to the Channel Islands. The trail parallels the coast for 0.3 miles, then curves inland. Climb steadily up the ridge, and cross over a minor side canyon to a view of the sculptured land forms in the interior of Leo Carrillo State Beach and the Arroyo Sequit drainage. At 1.4 miles, the encroaching vegetation narrows the winding road to a single track trail. Cross the county line and walk around a gate, continuing 300 yards ahead to a Y-fork. The left fork descends to PCH. Stay to the right, below a water tank on the right. At 2 miles the road/trail makes a left bend. On the bend is a footpath veering up the knoll to the right, our return route. Continue on the main trail, curving around the west flank of the knoll. Near the ridge, the uphill grade eases, reaching a trail sign. Continue to the ridge 150 yards ahead, with an awesome view of Boney Mountain Ridge. Leave the road and return on the trail to the right, climbing up the north face of the knoll. Cross over the 1,366-foot summit, and descend along the ridge to the junction with the road at the water tank. Return along the same route.

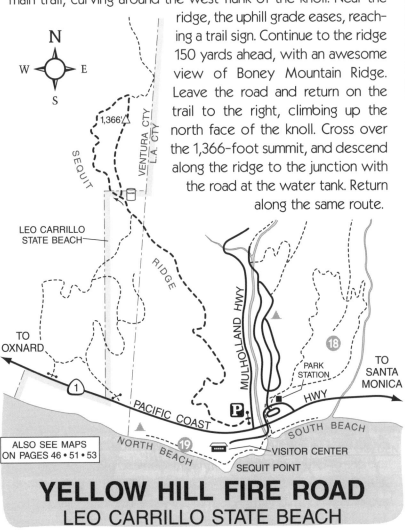

N

W ←○→ E

S

1,366'

SEQUIT

VENTURA CTY
L.A. CTY

LEO CARRILLO
STATE BEACH

RIDGE

MULHOLLAND HWY

TO
OXNARD

1

PACIFIC COAST

18

PARK
STATION

TO
SANTA
MONICA

P

HWY

SOUTH BEACH

ALSO SEE MAPS
ON PAGES 46 • 51 • 53

NORTH BEACH

19

VISITOR CENTER

SEQUIT POINT

YELLOW HILL FIRE ROAD
LEO CARRILLO STATE BEACH

Hike 18
Nicholas Flat and Willow Creek Loop
LEO CARRILLO STATE BEACH

Hiking distance: 2.5 mile loop
Hiking time: 1.3 hours
Elevation gain: 612 feet
Maps: U.S.G.S. Triunfo Pass
　　　　Santa Monica Mountains West Trail Map
　　　　Leo Carrillo State Beach map

Summary of hike: This loop hike in Leo Carrillo State Beach leads to Ocean Vista, a 612-foot bald knoll with great views of the Malibu coastline and Point Dume. The Willow Creek Trail traverses the east-facing hillside up Willow Creek Canyon to Ocean Vista. The hike returns along the Nicholas Flat Trail, one of the few trails connecting the Santa Monica Mountains to the Pacific Ocean.

Driving directions: From Santa Monica, drive 26 miles northbound on the Pacific Coast Highway (Highway 1) to the posted Leo Carrillo State Beach entrance and turn right. (The state park is 14 miles past Malibu Canyon Road and 8 miles past Kanan Dume Road.) Park in the day-use parking lot. A parking fee is required.

From the Pacific Coast Highway (Highway 1) and Las Posas Road in southeast Oxnard, drive 11.1 miles southbound to the posted Leo Carrillo State Beach entrance.

Hiking directions: The trailhead is 50 yards outside the park entrance station. Take the signed trail 100 yards northeast to a trail split. The loop begins at this junction. Take the right fork—the Willow Creek Trail—up the hillside and parallel to the ocean, heading east. At a half mile the trail curves north, traversing the hillside while overlooking the arroyo and Willow Creek. Three switchbacks lead aggressively up to a saddle and a signed four-way junction with the Nicholas Flat Trail. The left fork leads a quarter mile to Ocean Vista. After marveling at the views, return to the four-way junction and take the left (west) fork. Head downhill on the Nicholas Flat Trail across the grassy slopes above the park campground. Return to the junction near the trailhead.

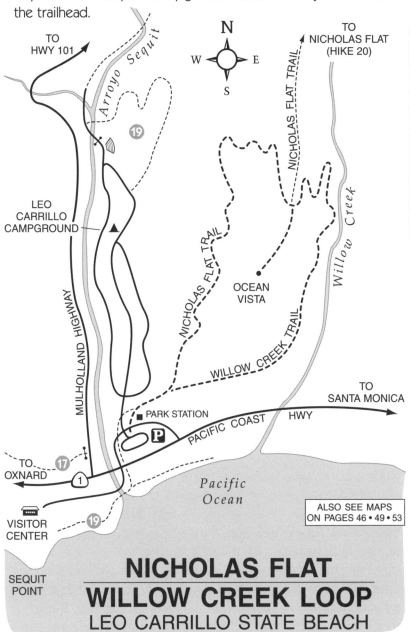

ALSO SEE MAPS
ON PAGES 46 • 49 • 53

NICHOLAS FLAT
WILLOW CREEK LOOP
LEO CARRILLO STATE BEACH

Hike 19
Lower Arroyo Sequit Trail and Sequit Point
LEO CARRILLO STATE BEACH

Hiking distance: 3 miles round trip
Hiking time: 1.5 hours
Elevation gain: 200 feet
Maps: U.S.G.S. Triunfo Pass
　　　　Leo Carrillo State Beach map

Summary of hike: Leo Carrillo State Beach is a 2,000-acre haven with a 1.5-mile stretch of coastline, mountain canyons, and steep chaparral-covered hillsides. The area was once inhabited by the Chumash Indians. The Lower Arroyo Sequit Trail leads into a cool, stream-fed canyon shaded with willow, sycamore, oak, and bay trees. The path ends in the deep-walled canyon by large multicolored boulders and the trickling stream. At the oceanfront, Sequit Point, a rocky bluff, juts out from the shoreline, dividing North Beach from South Beach. The weather-carved point has sea caves and coves, ocean-sculpted arches, tidepools, and pocket beaches.

Driving directions: Same as Hike 18.

Hiking directions: Hike north through the campground on the road past mature sycamores and oaks. Pass the amphitheater on the right to a gated road. Continue past the gate, crossing over the seasonal Arroyo Sequit to the end of the paved road. Take the footpath a hundred yards, and rock hop over the creek by a small grotto. Follow the path upstream along the east side of the creek. Recross the creek to the trail's end in a steep-walled box canyon with pools and large boulders. Retrace your steps to the amphitheater, and now bear left on the footpath. Cross to the east side of the creek and head through the forest canopy. Switchbacks and two sets of wooden steps lead to a flat above the canyon. Descend back to the campground road.

To reach Sequit Point, take the paved path under Highway 1

to the sandy beach. To the right (west), by the lifeguard station, are sandstone rock formations with caves, tunnels, a rock arch, tidepools, and a series of beach coves.

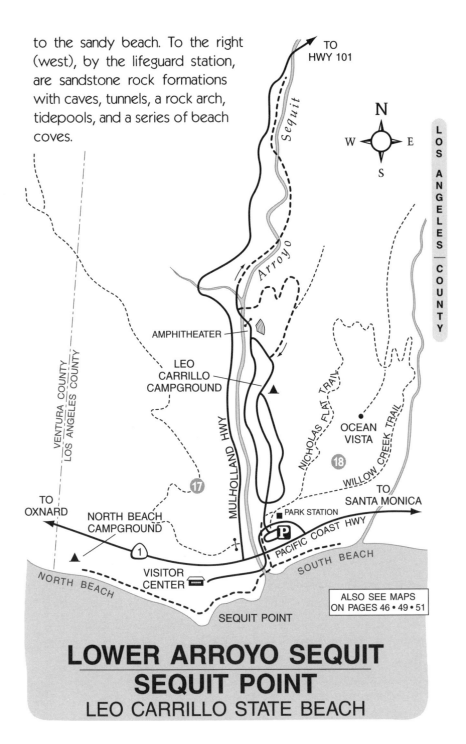

LOWER ARROYO SEQUIT
SEQUIT POINT
LEO CARRILLO STATE BEACH

Hike 20
Nicholas Flat
LEO CARRILLO STATE BEACH

Hiking distance: 2.5 mile double loop
Hiking time: 1.3 hours
Elevation gain: 100 feet
Maps: U.S.G.S. Triunfo Pass
Santa Monica Mountains West Trail Map
Leo Carrillo State Beach map

Summary of hike: Nicholas Flat, in the upper reaches of Leo Carrillo State Beach, is a grassy highland meadow with large oak trees, an old cattle pond, and sandstone outcroppings 1,700 feet above the sea. This hike skirts around Nicholas Flat with spectacular views of the ocean, San Nicholas Canyon, and the surrounding mountains. The Nicholas Flat Trail may be hiked 3.5 miles downhill to the Pacific Ocean, connecting to Hike 18.

Driving directions: From Santa Monica, drive 23.8 miles northbound on the Pacific Coast Highway (Highway 1) to Decker Road and turn right. (Decker Road is 11.8 miles past Malibu Canyon Road.) Continue 2.4 miles north to Decker School Road and turn left. Drive 1.5 miles to the road's end and park alongside the road.
From the Pacific Coast Highway (Highway 1) and Las Posas Road in southeast Oxnard, drive 13.3 miles southbound to Decker Road and turn left. Proceed with the directions above.

Hiking directions: Hike south past the gate and kiosk. Stay on the wide, oak-lined trail to a junction at 0.3 miles. Take the right fork, beginning the first loop. At 0.6 miles is another junction. Again take the right fork—the Meadows Trail. Continue past the Malibu Springs Trail on the right to Vista Point, where there are great views into the canyons. The trail curves south to a junction with the Nicholas Flat Trail, leading to Leo Carrillo State Beach. Take the left fork around the perimeter of the flat. A trail on the right leads to another vista point. Complete the

first loop at 1.8 miles. Take the trail to the right at two succes-
sive junctions to a pond. Follow along the pond through the
meadow, completing the second loop. Return to the trailhead.

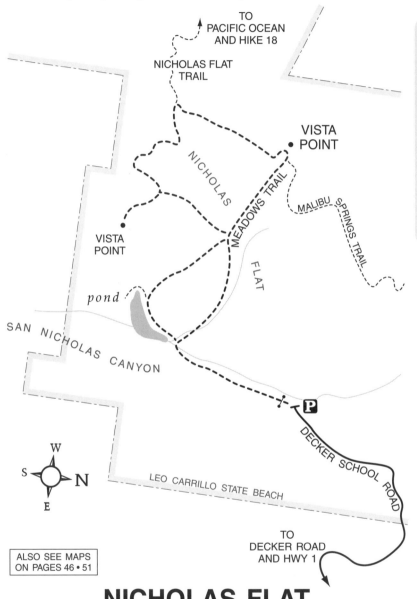

NICHOLAS FLAT
LEO CARRILLO STATE BEACH

Hike 21
Charmlee County Park
Open 8:00 a.m. to sunset daily

Hiking distance: 3 mile loop
Hiking time: 1.5 hours
Elevation gain: 600 feet
Maps: U.S.G.S. Triunfo Pass
Santa Monica Mountains West Trail Map
City of Malibu—Charmlee Natural Area map

Summary of hike: Perched on oceanfront cliffs 1,300 feet above the sea, Charmlee County Park has a magnificent bird's-eye view of the Malibu coastline. The 460-acre wilderness park was an old cattle ranch, purchased by Los Angeles County in 1968 and opened as a county park in 1981. A network of interconnecting footpaths and old ranch roads weave through expansive grassy meadows, oak and eucalyptus woodlands, mountain slopes, rocky ridges, and 1,250-foot bluffs overlooking the sea. The park has picnic areas and a nature center with plant exhibits.

Driving directions: From Santa Monica, drive 23.2 miles northbound on the Pacific Coast Highway (Highway 1) to Encinal Canyon Road and turn right. (Encinal Canyon Road is 11.2 miles past Malibu Canyon Road.) Continue 3.7 miles to the park entrance on the left. Drive 0.2 miles on the park road to the parking lot.

From the Pacific Coast Highway (Highway 1) and Las Posas Road in southeast Oxnard, drive 14 miles southbound to Encinal Canyon Road. Proceed with the directions above.

Hiking directions: Hike past the information board and picnic area on the wide trail. Pass a second picnic area on the left in an oak grove, and continue uphill to a three-way trail split. The middle trail is a short detour leading to an overlook set among rock formations and an old house foundation. Take the main trail to the left into the large grassy meadow. Two trails cross the meadow and rejoin at the south end—the main trail heads through the meadow while the right fork skirts the meadow's western edge. At the far end is an ocean overlook and a trail fork. Bear left past an old ranch reservoir, and pass two junctions to a 1,200-foot overlook on the right. Continue downhill, curving north through an oak grove to the unsigned Botany Trail, a narrow footpath on the right. The Botany Trail winds back to the picnic area and the trailhead.

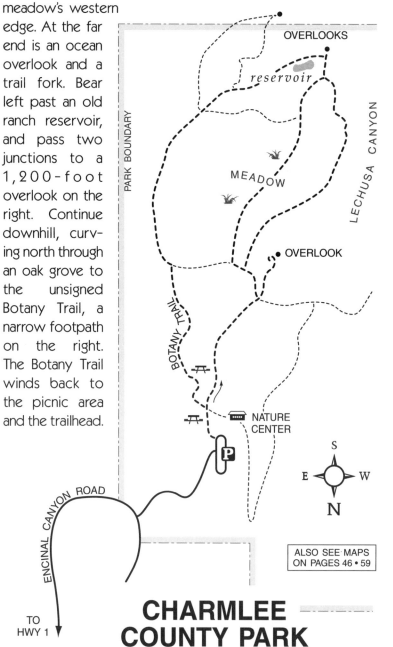

OVERLOOKS

reservoir

PARK BOUNDARY

LECHUSA CANYON

MEADOW

OVERLOOK

BOTANY TRAIL

NATURE CENTER

P

ENCINAL CANYON ROAD

TO HWY 1

S
E ⊕ W
N

ALSO SEE MAPS ON PAGES 46 • 59

CHARMLEE COUNTY PARK

Hike 22
El Matador, La Piedra and El Pescador State Beaches
ROBERT H. MEYER MEMORIAL STATE BEACH

Hiking distance: 2 miles round trip
Hiking time: 2 hours
Elevation gain: 100 feet for each hike
Maps: U.S.G.S. Triunfo Pass and Point Dume

Summary of hike: El Matador, La Piedra, and El Pescador State Beaches are three small oceanfront parks on the Malibu bluffs which comprise the Robert H. Meyer Memorial State Beach. The three pocket beaches are within a one-mile stretch, bounded by rocky points. Each park contains a blufftop parking lot, a picnic area with overlooks, a pretty beach strand, and a trail down the 100-foot eroded cliffs to the shoreline. Of the three, El Matador Beach is the largest and most scenic, with large rock formations, arches, and caves.

Driving directions: EL PESCADOR STATE PARK Heading northbound on the Pacific Coast Highway (Highway 1) from Santa Monica, drive 20 miles past Malibu Canyon Road and 6 miles past Kanan Dume Road to the posted turnoff on the left.
   From the Pacific Coast Highway (Highway 1) and Las Posas Road in southeast Oxnard, drive 13.4 miles southbound to the posted El Pescador State Beach on the right (oceanside). The turnoff is 2.3 miles south of Leo Carrillo State Beach and just south of Decker Road.
   LA PIEDRA STATE PARK is 0.2 miles east (southbound) from El Pescador State Park.
   EL MATADOR STATE PARK is 0.9 miles east (southbound) from El Pescador State Park.

Hiking directions: EL PESCADOR STATE BEACH (10 acres): Walk across the grassy field to the bluffs. The path begins from the west side of the park. Descend the bluffs to the east, dropping onto the sandy beach. The small beach pocket is bordered on each end by blufftop homes.

LA PIEDRA STATE BEACH (9 acres): A side path by the picnic tables leads to an overlook on the edge of the 100-foot bluffs. The main trail begins at the upper west end of the parking lot. Drop down the cliffs through a draw to a long, narrow, sandy beach with a rocky west end. To the east, the beach ends at a home on the point at the base of the cliffs.

EL MATADOR STATE BEACH (18 acres): Walk towards the 100-foot bluffs to a picnic area overlooking the ocean and adjacent beachfront homes. Take the path to the left, looping clockwise down the eroding cliffs. Two sets of stairs lead down to the gorgeous beach with offshore rock outcroppings and caves. When the tide is right, water swirls through the caves and sea stack tunnels in the rock formations. To the east, beyond the state park boundary, are private homes. If strolling to the east, stay below the high-tide water line to avoid property owner hassles.

LECHUZA POINT

ALSO SEE MAP ON PAGE 46

EL MATADOR
LA PIEDRA
EL PESCADOR
STATE BEACHES

Hike 23
Point Dume Natural Preserve

Hiking distance: 1.5 miles round trip
Hiking time: 45 minutes
Elevation gain: 200 feet
Maps: U.S.G.S. Point Dume

Summary of hike: Point Dume Natural Preserve is a 35-acre preserve on the northwest tip of Santa Monica Bay. The triangular-shaped sandstone headland juts out to sea, surrounded by water on three sides. From the 203-foot perch at the tip, views extend across Santa Monica Bay from Point Mugu to Palos Verdes. From mid-December through March, the summit is among the finest sites to observe the migrating gray whales en route from the Bering Sea to Baja California. On the west side of the point is Point Dume State Beach, a popular swimming, sunbathing, and tidepooling beach with a rocky shoreline. To the east, tucked beneath the 200-foot sandstone cliffs, is Dume Cove (locally known as Pirates Cove), a secluded, unofficial clothing-optional beach between two rocky points.

Driving directions: From Santa Monica, drive 20 miles northbound on the Pacific Coast Highway (Highway 1) to Westward Beach Road by Point Dume and turn left. (Westward Beach Road is 0.9 miles past Kanan Dume Road.) Turn left and drive 0.6 miles to the Point Dume State Beach entrance station. Continue 0.7 miles to the far south end of the parking lot. A parking fee is required.

For a second access point, just before reaching the beach entrance station, turn left on Birdview Avenue, and drive 1 mile to limited curbside parking spaces on the right. (Birdview Avenue becomes Cliffside Drive en route.)

Hiking directions: Walk towards the cliffs, past the trail-head gate, at the Point Dume Natural Preserve boundary. Wind up the hill on the footpath to a junction. The left fork leads to Birdview Avenue in a residential neighborhood. Stay to the right to a second junction. The right fork follows the ridge to a rocky point and ends at a fenced overlook. Return to the junction and take the other fork. A short distance ahead is a 4-way junction. The left fork loops around the terraced flat with coastal sage scrub to Birdview Avenue; it also connects with the beach access to Dume Cove. The right fork leads uphill to the summit, 203 feet above the ocean. The middle fork follows a board-walk to a platform overlook. From the platform, a sandy path continues a short distance around to the point. Return to the beach access, and descend on the trail and stairs to Dume (Pirates) Cove at the base of the cliffs. At low tide, explore the tidepools and walk along the rocky shoreline northeast into Paradise Cove, a privately run, crescent-shaped beach with a small pier and concessions.

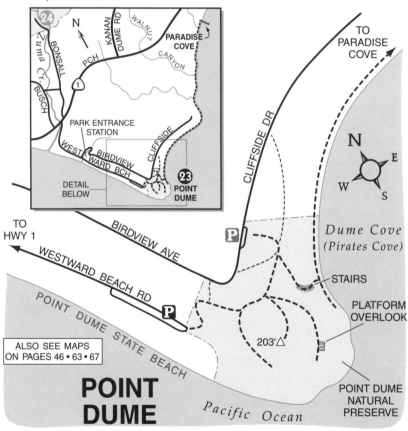

Hike 24
Zuma Loop Trail
ZUMA/TRANCAS CANYONS: Lower Zuma Canyon

Hiking distance: 1.7 mile loop
Hiking time: 1 hour
Elevation gain: 250 feet
Maps: U.S.G.S. Point Dume
Santa Monica Mountains West Trail Map
N.P.S. Zuma/Trancas Canyons map

Summary of hike: Zuma Canyon is one of the few canyons in the Santa Monica Mountains that is accessible only to foot and horse traffic. There are no paved roads. This hike begins on the Zuma Canyon Trail in Lower Zuma Canyon. The trail heads up the drainage parallel to Zuma Creek past lush riparian vegetation, oak, willow, and sycamore trees. The hike returns on the Zuma Loop Trail above the canyon floor, traversing the east-facing hillside overlooking the canyon and the ocean.

Driving directions: From Santa Monica, drive 21 miles northbound on the Pacific Coast Highway (Highway 1) to Bonsall Drive and turn right. (The turnoff is one mile past Kanan Dume Road.) Continue one mile north to the trailhead parking area at road's end. The last 200 yards are on an unpaved lane.

Hiking directions: From the end of the road, hike north past the trailhead gate on the Zuma Canyon Trail. At 0.2 miles is a junction with the Zuma Loop Trail. Go straight on the Zuma Canyon Trail past oak and sycamore trees. Continue past the junction with the Ocean View Trail on the right (Hike 25), cross Zuma Creek, and head to a junction with the Canyon View Trail. Bear left and remain close to the creek. At 0.7 miles, cross Zuma Creek to a junction. To add an additional 1.4 miles to the hike, take the right fork 0.7 miles up the canyon, crossing the creek several times to the trail's end. Return to the junction, and take the Zuma Loop Trail to the west, traversing the hillside. Follow the ridge south, bearing left at three separate trail forks before returning down to the canyon floor and completing the loop. Take the right fork back to the trailhead.

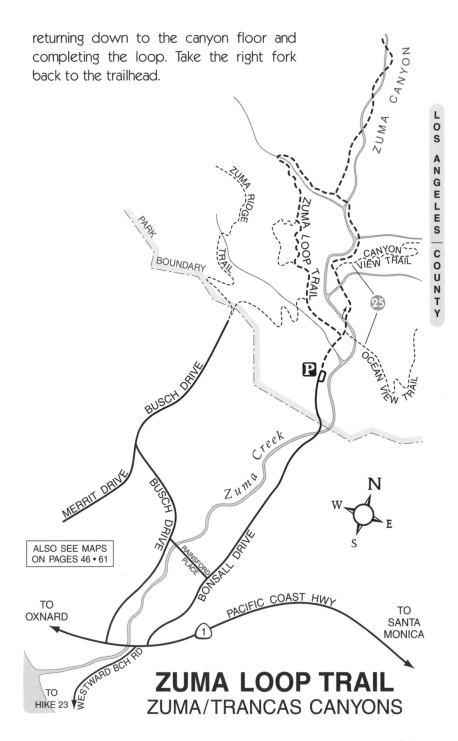

ALSO SEE MAPS
ON PAGES 46 • 61

ZUMA LOOP TRAIL
ZUMA/TRANCAS CANYONS

Hike 25
Ocean View—Canyon View Loop
ZUMA/TRANCAS CANYONS: Lower Zuma Canyon

Hiking distance: 3.1 miles round trip
Hiking time: 1.5 hours
Elevation gain: 600 feet
Maps: U.S.G.S. Point Dume
        Santa Monica Mountains West Trail Map
        N.P.S. Zuma/Trancas Canyons map

Summary of hike: Zuma Canyon remains a beautiful, natural gorge with minimal development in Lower Zuma Canyon. The perennial stream makes its way down the canyon floor, reaching the ocean at the west end of Point Dume (Hike 23). From the parking area, a trail follows the canyon bottom and links to a network of hiking trails. This hike ascends the eastern hillside on the Ocean View Trail and returns back to the canyon on the Canyon View Trail. Throughout the hike are great views of Point Dume, the coastline, and upper Zuma Canyon.

Driving directions: Same as Hike 24.

Hiking directions: From the mouth of the canyon, head north up the canyon floor for 0.2 miles to a signed junction. The Zuma Canyon Loop (Hike 24) curves left. Stay on the canyon bottom 30 yards to the posted Ocean View Trail. Bear right, cross a rocky streambed, and ascend the east canyon wall. Wind up the hillside to views of Point Dume and the ocean, reaching the ridge at 1.3 miles. At the summit are sweeping coastal views that extend (on clear days) to Palos Verdes, Point Mugu, and Catalina. The Ocean View Trail ends at a T-junction, but the ocean views continue throughout the hike. Bear left 0.1 miles on the unpaved Kanan Edison Road to a junction with the Canyon View Trail. Curve left and follow the ridge across the head of the small side canyon. Weave down the hillside to the canyon floor and a junction at 2.6 miles. Bear left on the Zuma Canyon Trail and walk down canyon. Parallel the small stream past laurel sumac bushes and sycamore trees. Complete the loop and return to the trailhead.

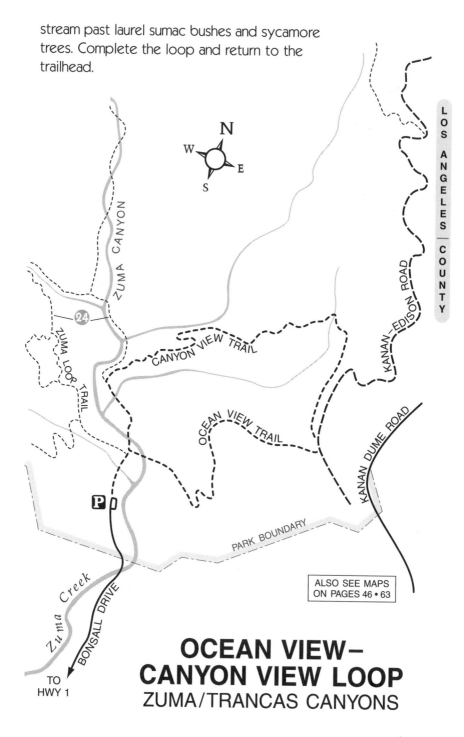

**OCEAN VIEW–
CANYON VIEW LOOP**
ZUMA/TRANCAS CANYONS

Hike 26
Escondido Falls

Hiking distance: 4.2 miles round trip
Hiking time: 2 hours
Elevation gain: 300 feet
Maps: U.S.G.S. Point Dume
       Santa Monica Mountains East Trail Map

Summary of hike: Escondido Falls is a 200-foot multi-tiered cataract deep within the Escondido Canyon Natural Area. The upper cascade can be spotted during the hike, but the trail ends at the base of the lower falls in a box canyon. The falls tumbles 50 feet into a shallow pool, cascading off limestone cliffs into a mossy fern grotto. The hike to the falls begins on a winding, paved residential road due to trail access problems. In less than a mile, a footpath descends into the forested canyon. In the shade of oaks, willows, and sycamores, the canyon trail follows a year-round creek to the waterfall.

Driving directions: From Santa Monica, drive 16.5 miles northbound on the Pacific Coast Highway (Highway 1) to Winding Way and turn right. (Winding Way is 4.5 miles past Malibu Canyon Road.) The signed parking lot is on the left side of Winding Way.

Hiking directions: Hike north up Winding Way past some beautiful homes and ocean vistas on the south-facing slope. At 0.8 miles, leave the road on the well-defined trail, crossing the meadow to the left. Hike downhill into Escondido Canyon and cross the creek. After crossing, take the left fork upstream. (The right fork leads to Latigo Canyon.) Continue up the nearly level canyon trail beside the creek. The forested trail crosses the creek a few more times. After the fifth crossing, Escondido Falls comes into view. The trail ends by a shallow pool surrounded by travertine rock at the base of the waterfall. Return by reversing your route. (The upper falls is on private property and access is not permitted.)

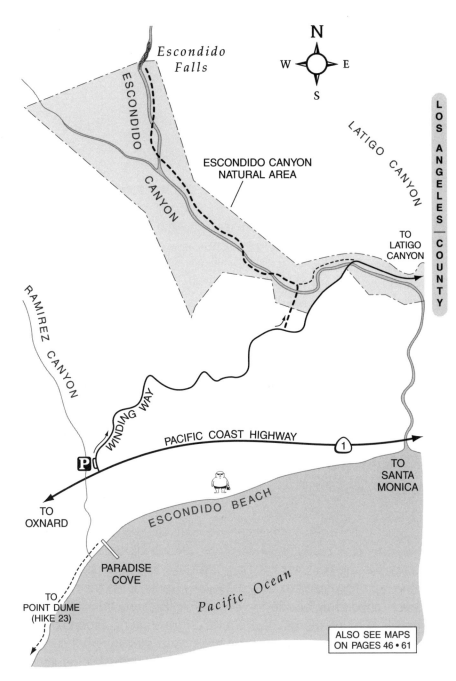

Escondido Falls

N **W** **E** **S**

ESCONDIDO CANYON
NATURAL AREA

ESCONDIDO CANYON

LATIGO CANYON

TO
LATIGO
CANYON

LOS ANGELES — COUNTY

RAMIREZ CANYON

WINDING WAY

PACIFIC COAST HIGHWAY ①

P

TO
SANTA
MONICA

TO
OXNARD

ESCONDIDO BEACH

PARADISE
COVE

TO
POINT DUME
(HIKE 23)

Pacific Ocean

ALSO SEE MAPS
ON PAGES 46 • 61

ESCONDIDO FALLS

Hike 27
Rising Sun—Solstice Canyon Loop
SOLSTICE CANYON

Hiking distance: 2.8-mile loop
Hiking time: 1.5 hours
Elevation gain: 400 feet
Maps: U.S.G.S. Point Dume and Malibu Beach
      N.P.S. Solstice Canyon map
      Santa Monica Mountains East Trail Map

Summary of hike: The hike up Solstice Canyon leads to Tropical Terrace, the ruins of a home built in the 1950s and destroyed by fire in 1982. The stone courtyard, garden terraces, stairways, and exotic tropical plants still remain. Near the ruins is Solstice Canyon Falls cascading 30 feet over sandstone rocks. The Rising Sun Trail traverses the east wall of Solstice Canyon. The undulating path overlooks the lush canyon to the Pacific Ocean. The hike returns along the canyon floor parallel to Solstice Creek, passing through oak and walnut groves, grassy meadows, and picnic areas.

Driving directions: From Santa Monica, drive 14.3 miles northbound on the Pacific Coast Highway (Highway 1) to Corral Canyon Road and turn right. (Corral Canyon Road is 2.3 miles past Malibu Canyon Road.) Continue 0.2 miles to the gated entrance on the left. Turn left and drive 0.3 miles to the parking lot at road's end.

Hiking directions: Hike north up the steps past the TRW Trailhead sign. Wind up the hillside to a service road. Take the road uphill to the right to the TRW buildings, now home for the Santa Monica Mountains Conservancy. The Rising Sun Trail begins to the right of the second building. Long, wide switchbacks lead up to the east ridge of Solstice Canyon. Follow the ridge north towards the back of the canyon, and descend through lush vegetation. At the canyon floor, cross the creek to the ruins. Take the path upstream to the waterfalls and pools. After exploring, return on the service road parallel to Solstice Creek. A half mile down canyon is the Keller House, a stone cottage built in 1865. Bear left at a road split, cross a wooden bridge, and return to the trailhead.

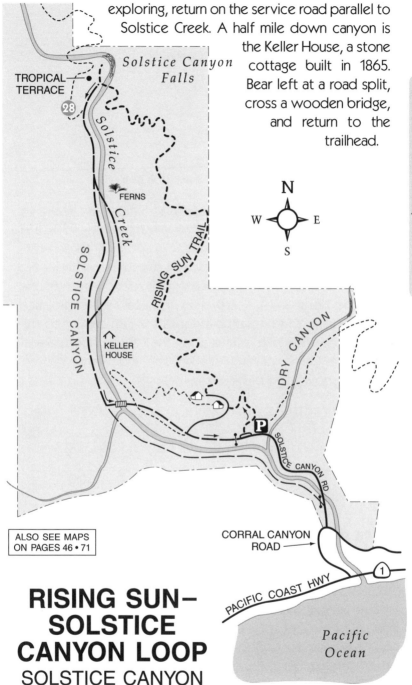

ALSO SEE MAPS
ON PAGES 46 • 71

RISING SUN–
SOLSTICE
CANYON LOOP
SOLSTICE CANYON

Hike 28
Sostomo—Deer Valley Loop
SOLSTICE CANYON

Hiking distance: 6.2 miles round trip
Hiking time: 3 hours
Elevation gain: 1,100 feet
Maps: U.S.G.S. Point Dume
        N.P.S. Solstice Canyon map
        Santa Monica Mountains East Trail Map

Summary of hike: The Sostomo-Deer Valley Loop ascends the west wall of Solstice Canyon to a 1,200-foot ridge. The trail winds through chaparral and coastal sage with stream crossings, oak woodlands, and grassy meadows. Sweeping vistas above Point Dume extend across Santa Monica Bay. The Sostomo-Deer Valley Loop is accessed by the Solstice Canyon Trail (Hike 27), which follows Solstice Creek along the canyon floor through meadows, picnic areas, oak and walnut groves, and past the historic Keller House, a stone building dating back to 1865.

Driving directions: Same as Hike 27.

Hiking directions: Take the posted Solstice Canyon Trail, and follow the paved road under sycamore trees alongside the creek. Cross a wood bridge to the west side of the creek at 0.2 miles. Continue up canyon past the historic Keller House. Just beyond the house is a trail split. The right fork leaves the main road and meanders through an oak grove, crossing the creek twice before rejoining the road. At 1.2 miles, just shy of Tropical Terrace, is the posted Sostomo Trail. Bear left on the footpath, and begin ascending the west canyon wall. Climb at a moderate grade to magnificent views of Solstice Canyon. Rock hop over the creek in a narrow gorge. Wind up the canyon wall, passing the remnants of a home and chimney. At the head of the canyon is a towering sedimentary rock monolith. The trail skirts the park boundary and curves left before reaching the spectacular outcropping. Cross the creek again, passing the shell of a sturdy rock house. Climb to a junction with the Deer Valley Loop. Begin the loop to the right, leading to an open, grassy flat where the trail levels off. At an unpaved road, bear left for 50 yards and return to the footpath on the left. The sweeping coastal views extend across Santa Monica Bay, including a bird's-eye view of Point Dume. Switchback sharply left at the trail sign, and return on the lower loop. The Rising Sun Trail (Hike 27) can be seen across the canyon. Complete the loop and return by retracing your steps.

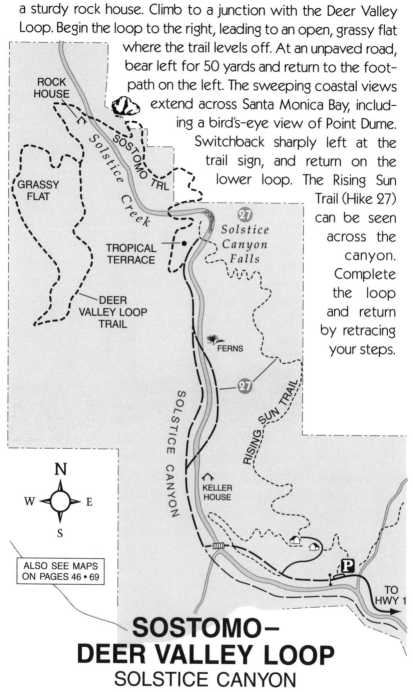

ROCK HOUSE

GRASSY FLAT

Solstice Creek

SOSTOMO TRL

27

Solstice Canyon Falls

TROPICAL TERRACE

DEER VALLEY LOOP TRAIL

FERNS

27

SOLSTICE CANYON

RISING SUN TRAIL

KELLER HOUSE

N
W   E
S

ALSO SEE MAPS ON PAGES 46 • 69

TO HWY 1

P

SOSTOMO–
DEER VALLEY LOOP
SOLSTICE CANYON

Hike 29
Malibu Bluffs Recreation Area and Community Park

Hiking distance: 2 mile loop
Hiking time: 1 hour
Elevation gain: 100 feet
Maps: U.S.G.S. Malibu Beach
Santa Monica Mountains East Trail Map

Summary of hike: Malibu Bluffs Recreation Area comprises 90 acres on the bluffs between the Pacific Coast Highway and Malibu Road, directly opposite of Pepperdine University and Malibu Canyon Road. The 100-foot bluffs rise above Amarillo Beach and Puerco Beach. Five public stairways (which adjoin private property) lead down to the shoreline from the base of the bluffs. The trails begin from the spacious lawns in Malibu Bluffs Community Park, a park with picnic facilities, ball fields, and a free parking lot.

Driving directions: From Santa Monica, drive 12 miles northbound on the Pacific Coast Highway (Highway 1) to Malibu Canyon Road by Pepperdine University. Turn left into the posted Malibu Bluffs Community Park parking lot.

Hiking directions: From the northwest corner of the parking lot, take the path closest to the Pacific Coast Highway and head west. Cross the meadow, passing a pocket of eucalyptus trees on the right, to a T-junction at the edge of deep Marie Canyon. The right fork exits the parkland to PCH, just east of John Tyler Drive. Bear left and follow the east ridge of the canyon to the bluffs closest to the ocean. Curve left along the edge of the bluffs to a junction. The right fork descends to the oceanfront homes and coastal access stairways at Malibu Road. Bear left and cross the footbridge over a minor drainage to another junction. The right fork gradually climbs to a picnic area at the southwest corner of Malibu Bluffs Community Park. Take the left fork 100 yards, following the east side of the gully. Two switchbacks zigzag up the hillside to great views of Pepperdine University and the Santa Monica Mountains. Continue to a trail fork. The left fork heads straight to the trailhead. Go to the right, climbing to a picnic area and paved path. Follow the blufftop path to the left and circle the park, passing the ball fields while overlooking Malibu Point (Hike 30). The path ends on the park road. Return along the road to the left.

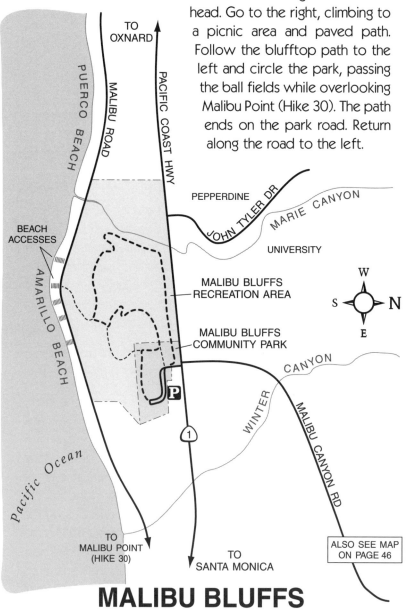

TO
OXNARD

PUERCO BEACH

MALIBU ROAD

PACIFIC COAST HWY

BEACH
ACCESSES

AMARILLO BEACH

Pacific Ocean

PEPPERDINE

JOHN TYLER DR.

MARIE CANYON

UNIVERSITY

MALIBU BLUFFS
RECREATION AREA

MALIBU BLUFFS
COMMUNITY PARK

CANYON

WINTER

MALIBU CANYON RD

P

1

W

S — N

E

TO
MALIBU POINT
(HIKE 30)

TO
SANTA MONICA

ALSO SEE MAP
ON PAGE 46

MALIBU BLUFFS
RECREATION AREA and COMMUNITY PARK

Hike 30
Malibu Lagoon State Beach
MALIBU POINT

Hiking distance: 1.5 miles round trip
Hiking time: 1 hour
Elevation gain: Level
Maps: U.S.G.S. Malibu Beach

Summary of hike: Malibu Lagoon State Beach encompasses 167 acres in the heart of Malibu, with a brackish lagoon at the mouth of perennial Malibu Creek and nearly a mile of ocean frontage. The sand-barred lagoon, just off Malibu Point, is a resting and feeding estuary for more than 200 species of migrating and native birds on the Pacific Flyway. The state beach includes a museum; 35-acre Surfrider Beach, popularized by surfing movies in the 1950s and 1960s; and Malibu Pier, a 700-foot long pier in a cove called Kellers Shelter. The historic pier dates back to 1903 and was rebuilt in 1946. To the west of Malibu Point is the exclusive Malibu Colony gated community. Nature trails meander to the beach and around the lagoon.

Driving directions: From Santa Monica, drive 11 miles north-bound on the Pacific Coast Highway (Highway 1) to Cross Creek Road by the posted Malibu Lagoon State Beach turnoff. (The turnoff is 1.1 miles south of Malibu Canyon Road.) Turn left into the park, passing the entrance station to the parking lot. A parking fee is required.

Hiking directions: Take the paved path, crossing a series of bridges over the wetlands and lagoon. The path ends at the sandy beach on Malibu Point at the north end of Surfrider Beach. From here there are several walking options. Stroll south along Surfrider Beach to the Malibu Pier. Head north from Malibu Point along Malibu Beach in front of the Malibu Colony homes. (On this route, stay below the high-tide water line to avoid property owner hassles.) The third choice is to loop around the lagoon on the sandy beach.

Back at the trailhead on the far end of the parking lot, a bridge crosses an arm of the lagoon on estuary trails to a junction. The right fork leads through tall brush to a small opening on the lagoon. The left fork winds through the brush under PCH to the main lagoon channel.

TO OXNARD

MALIBU RD

Pacific Ocean

MALIBU DR

MALIBU COLONY DR

MALIBU COLONY

MALIBU BEACH

W
S — N
E

1

ENTRANCE STATION

P

CROSS CREEK RD

Malibu Creek

MALIBU POINT

Malibu Lagoon

SERRA RD

MALIBU CREEK STATE PARK

SURFRIDER BEACH

ADAMSON HOUSE

PACIFIC COAST HWY

MALIBU LAGOON STATE BEACH

KELLERS

SHELTER

MALIBU PIER

ALSO SEE MAP ON PAGE 46

MALIBU LAGOON STATE BEACH
MALIBU POINT

TO SANTA MONICA

Hike 31
Parker Mesa Overlook
from TOPANGA STATE PARK

Hiking distance: 6 miles round trip
Hiking time: 3 hours
Elevation gain: 800 feet
Maps: U.S.G.S. Topanga
Santa Monica Mountains East Trail Map

map
next page

Summary of hike: This hike follows the East Topanga Fire Road along the ridge dividing Topanga Canyon and Santa Ynez Canyon. There are spectacular views into both canyons, including numerous ravines and enormous slabs of sandstone. This hike begins in Topanga State Park at Trippet Ranch (the park headquarters) and heads south. The trail leads to Parker Mesa Overlook, a barren knoll overlooking Topanga Beach, Santa Monica Bay, Pacific Palisades, and Santa Monica. The overlook can also be accessed from the south (Hike 32).

Driving directions: From Santa Monica, drive 4 miles northbound on the Pacific Coast Highway (Highway 1) to Topanga Canyon Boulevard and turn right. Continue 4.6 miles to Entrada Road on the right and turn right again. Drive 0.7 miles and turn left, following the posted state park signs. Turn left again in 0.3 miles into the Topanga State Park parking lot.

From the Ventura Freeway (Highway 101) in Woodland Hills, exit on Topanga Canyon Boulevard, and drive 7.6 miles south to Entrada Drive. Turn left and follow the posted state park signs to the parking lot.

Hiking directions: Head southeast on the signed trail towards Eagle Rock to a fire road. Bear left up the road to a junction at 0.2 miles. The left fork leads to Eagle Rock. Take the right fork on the East Topanga Fire Road past a grove of coastal oaks. Continue uphill to a ridge and a bench with panoramic views, from Topanga Canyon to the Pacific Ocean. A short distance ahead, the trail crosses a narrow ridge overlooking Santa

Ynez Canyon and its tilted sandstone slabs. Follow the ridge south, with alternating views of both canyons. At 2.5 miles is a junction with a trail on the right. The main trail (left) leads to Paseo Miramar (Hike 32). Leave the fire road, and take the right trail a half mile to Parker Mesa Overlook at the trail's end. After enjoying the views, return to Trippet Ranch along the same route. Or, for a one-way, 5.5-mile shuttle hike, combine Hikes 31 and 32.

Hike 32
Parker Mesa Overlook
from PASEO MIRAMAR

Hiking distance: 5 miles round trip
Hiking time: 2.5 hours
Elevation gain: 1,200 feet
Maps: U.S.G.S. Topanga
       Santa Monica Mountains East Trail Map

map
next page

Summary of hike: The hike to Parker Mesa Overlook from Paseo Miramar has spectacular vistas along the trail. The trail follows a ridge separating Santa Ynez Canyon and Los Liones Canyon. There are views from Venice to Malibu and from West Los Angeles to Topanga. The Parker Mesa Overlook (also known as the Topanga Overlook) is a barren knoll overlooking Santa Monica Bay to Palos Verdes and, on clear days, Catalina Island.

Driving directions: From Santa Monica, drive 3 miles north-bound on the Pacific Coast Highway (Highway 1) to Sunset Boulevard. Turn right and drive 0.3 miles to Paseo Miramar. Turn left and drive about one mile to the end of the road and park.

Hiking directions: Hike north past the fire road gate as the road climbs along the ridge. Pass the Los Liones Trail on the left. Continue along the hillside overlooking Santa Ynez Canyon to a junction at two miles. Leave the fire road and take the trail to the left, heading south. The trail ends a half mile ahead at the

Parker Mesa Overlook, a bald knoll overlooking the Pacific Ocean. (The main fire road leads 2.5 miles further to Trippet Ranch—Hike 31.) After enjoying the views at the overlook, return along the same trail.

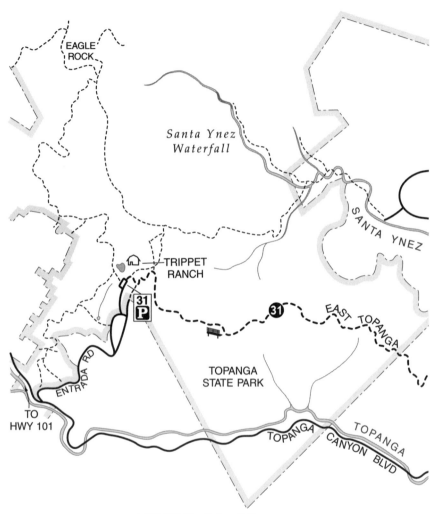

HIKES 31•32
PARKER MESA OVERLOOK
from TOPANGA STATE PARK
and PASEO MIRAMAR

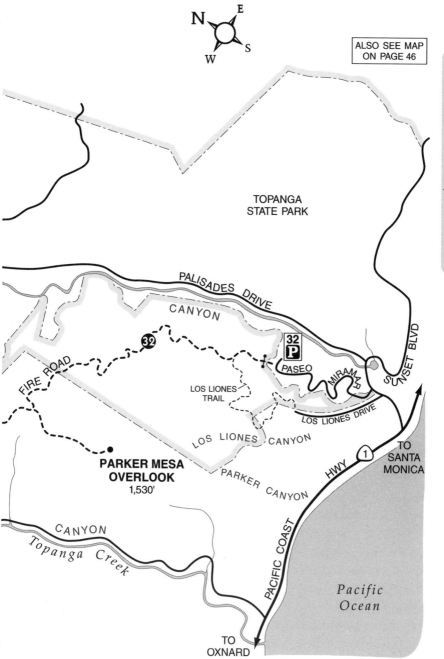

N E W S

ALSO SEE MAP
ON PAGE 46

LOS ANGELES COUNTY

TOPANGA
STATE PARK

PALISADES DRIVE

CANYON

FIRE ROAD

32

32
P

PASEO

MIRAMAR

SUNSET BLVD

LOS LIONES
TRAIL

LOS LIONES DRIVE

LOS LIONES CANYON

PARKER MESA
OVERLOOK
1,530'

PARKER CANYON

HWY

1

TO
SANTA
MONICA

CANYON

Topanga Creek

PACIFIC COAST

Pacific
Ocean

TO
OXNARD

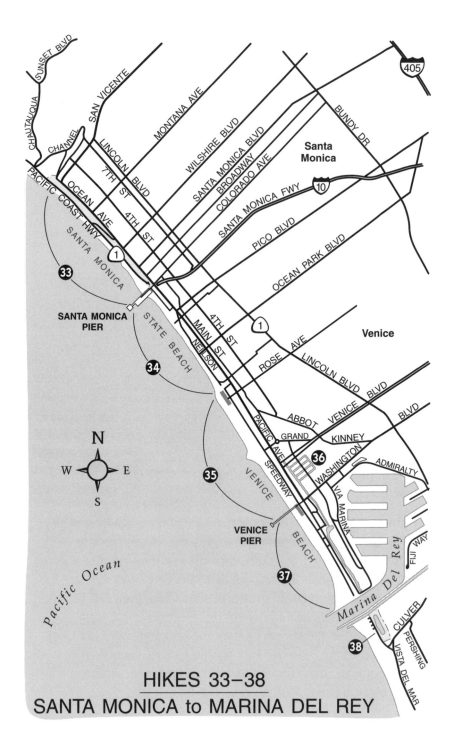

HIKES 33–38
SANTA MONICA to MARINA DEL REY

Hike 33
Palisades Park and Santa Monica Pier

Hiking distance: 3.5 miles round trip
Hiking time: 2 hours
Elevation gain: 100 feet
Maps: U.S.G.S. Topanga and Beverly Hills

map
next page

L
O
S

A
N
G
E
L
E
S

C
O
U
N
T
Y

Summary of hike: Palisades Park is perched on the eroding 100-foot bluffs above the Pacific Coast Highway, overlooking Santa Monica State Beach, the Santa Monica Pier, and the entire bay. The 26-acre park stretches 1.6 miles between Ocean Avenue and the sandstone cliffs. The gorgeous landscaped grounds are filled with palm, oak, and eucalyptus trees lining the paved and natural paths. Throughout the park are gardens with exotic and native plants, benches, and a few gazebos. A pedestrian bridge and stairway connect the park to the wide, sandy beach. The south end of the park has direct access onto the Santa Monica Pier.

Driving directions: Palisades Park is on the oceanfront bluffs in Santa Monica. The 1.6-mile-long park is located at the west end of Colorado Avenue, Santa Monica Boulevard, Wilshire Boulevard, Montana Avenue, and San Vicente Boulevard. Park along the oceanfront park in an available metered parking space. (For alternate parking, see Hike 34.)

Hiking directions: Begin the hike by strolling along the bluffs on the parallel paths, enjoying the vistas, people, and landscaping. From the south end of the park, at Colorado Avenue, bear right and head out onto the Santa Monica Pier. To return, descend steps on the north side of the pier, and follow the paved boardwalk 400 yards to the bridge crossing over PCH. Cross the bridge and climb the eroding cliffs on brick steps, reentering Palisades Park by the historic cannon.

To continue from the Santa Monica Pier, hike south on the Santa Monica Beach Promenade (Hike 34).

100 Great Hikes - **81**

Hike 34
Santa Monica Pier to Venice Beach

Hiking distance: 2.5 miles round trip
Hiking time: 1.5 hours
Elevation gain: Level
Maps: U.S.G.S. Beverly Hills and Venice

Summary of hike: The Santa Monica Pier sits beneath sandstone bluffs at the foot of Colorado Avenue in downtown Santa Monica. The landmark pier dates back to the early 1900s as a privately owned amusement center. It is still an amusement park, with an historic turn-of-the-century carousel, a ferris wheel, arcades, souvenir shops, food vendors, and pier fishing. Stairways from the north, south, and east sides of the pier descend onto Santa Monica State Beach. The state beach is a broad stretch of white sand stretching 3 miles from Chautauqua Boulevard to Venice Beach. Along the backside of the beach are a bicycle trail and a walking path. The South Bay Bicycle Trail extends over 20 miles, from Will Rogers State Beach south to Redondo Beach at the base of Palos Verdes (Hike 39).

Driving directions: From downtown Santa Monica, take Colorado Avenue west to Ocean Avenue. Cross Ocean Avenue onto the Santa Monica Pier. Park on the pier in the lots to the left.

Hiking directions: Before hiking the Santa Monica Beach Promenade, walk out on the pier past the ferris wheel, roller coaster, bumper cars, arcades, and curio shops to view the ocean and coastline from the end of the pier. Return to the parking lot, and descend the wood steps to the promenade. Follow the wide, paved path south (right), passing old historic buildings and the original Muscle Beach. Just past the west end of Pico Boulevard at Bay Street, the walking path curves right and continues parallel to the biking path. At 1.2 miles from the pier, the promenade connects with Ocean Front Walk at the north end of the Venice Beach Boardwalk. This is the turnaround spot. Return by retracing your route, or walk to the shoreline and return along the water.

To hike further, continue south through Venice Beach (Hike 35) or north through Palisades Park (Hike 33).

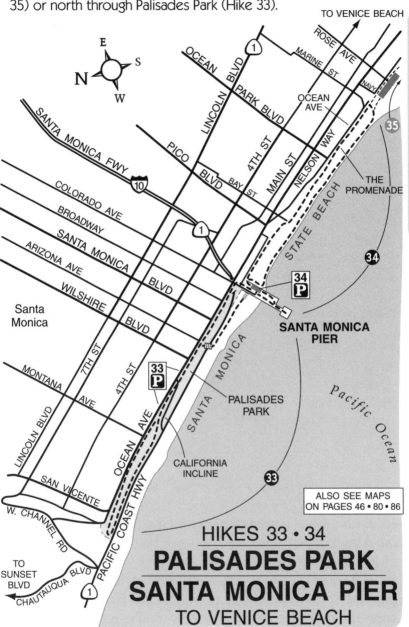

HIKES 33 • 34
PALISADES PARK
SANTA MONICA PIER
TO VENICE BEACH

Hike 35
Venice Beach

Hiking distance: 3 miles round trip
Hiking time: 2 hours
Elevation gain: Level
Maps: U.S.G.S. Venice

map
next page

Summary of hike: Venice Beach is a unique wedge of Los Angeles between Ocean Park (in Santa Monica) and the Marina Del Rey Harbor Channel. The famous Venice Beach Boardwalk is on Ocean Front Walk, an asphalt walkway that runs parallel to the back end of the wide, sandy beach. It extends south from Navy Street to the Venice Pier at the foot of Washington Boulevard. Winding through the sand is the 20-mile South Bay Bicycle Trail. The 1.5-mile promenade, built in 1905, is lined with beachfront businesses, cafes, hawkers, vendors, bodybuilders, musicians, comedians, artists, jugglers, fortune-tellers, dancers, drunks, hiking book publishers, panhandlers, spectators, and a vast array of other unique characters. The calm of the ocean is only steps away from the endless parade of people.

Driving directions: Venice Beach can be accessed from numerous east—west streets, including Washington Boulevard, Venice Boulevard, Windward Avenue, and Rose Avenue. This hike begins from the north end of Venice Beach, off of Rose Avenue. From the Santa Monica (10) Freeway in Santa Monica, exit on Lincoln Boulevard. Head 1.4 miles south to Rose Avenue. Turn right and follow Rose Avenue 0.9 miles into the Venice Beach oceanfront parking lot. A parking fee is required.

Hiking directions: From the north end of Venice Beach, walk south along the boardwalk, passing cafes and beautiful old brick buildings. Stroll through the zoo of humanity, marveling at the diverse circus. At 1 mile is the Venice Pavilion and outdoor roller skating area on the right. To the left is Windward Avenue, showcasing massive murals and charming Italian-style buildings with colonnades, dating back to 1905. Just past Windward

Avenue are paddle tennis courts, basketball courts, and an outdoor weight-lifting arena known as Muscle Beach (named after the historical Muscle Beach south of the Santa Monica Pier). The active, theatrical portion of the boardwalk ends at 1.5 miles by Venice Pier, a 1,100-foot pier at the west end of Washington Boulevard. This is the turnaround spot. Return along the boardwalk or go to the shoreline and return along the sea.

To extend the hike, continue south to the mouth of the Marina Del Rey Harbor Channel 1.1 miles ahead (Hike 37), north along Ocean Front Walk (Hike 34), or 2 blocks inland to the Venice Canals (Hike 36).

Hike 36
The Venice Canals

Hiking distance: 1 mile or more
Hiking time: Variable
Elevation gain: Level
Maps: U.S.G.S. Venice
       City of Venice map

map
next page

Summary of hike: The Venice Canals are located between Venice Boulevard and Washington Boulevard, two blocks inland from Venice Beach. In 1904, Abbot Kinney purchased 160 acres of coastal marshland, part of the Ballona Creek wetlands, to develop a new cultural center. He dreamed and developed "Venice in America," a seaside resort recreating the canals of Venice, Italy, with lagoons, arched Venetian-style bridges, gondolas imported from Italy, and a network of interconnected canals. What remains are six interwoven water canals flowing through a charming residential neighborhood, with landscaped walkways, diverse architecture, and 14 bridges. Canoes, paddle boats, and ducks grace the waterways, adding to an enchanting and unique experience.

Driving directions: From the San Diego Freeway / Interstate 405 in Culver City, take the Washington Boulevard exit, and drive 3.5 miles west towards the ocean to Dell Avenue.

The Venice Canals are located near the Pacific Coast between Washington Boulevard and Venice Boulevard, two blocks east of Pacific Avenue, which parallels the ocean. Dell Avenue crosses over the canals via four arched bridges. Park on Dell Avenue anywhere along the residential street.

Hiking directions: Walking paths border the canals on each side. Fourteen bridges span

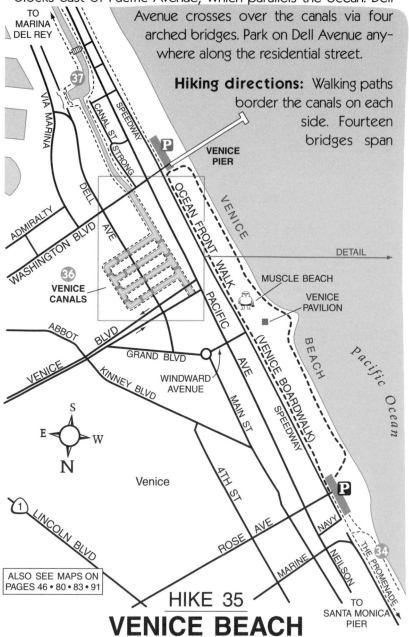

TO
MARINA
DEL REY

37

TO MARINA
DEL REY

VIA MARINA

CANAL ST

SPEEDWAY

STRONG

DELL

ADMIRALTY

WASHINGTON BLVD

AVE

36

VENICE
CANALS

ABBOT

BLVD

VENICE

KINNEY BLVD

GRAND BLVD

WINDWARD
AVENUE

P

VENICE
PIER

OCEAN FRONT WALK

VENICE

DETAIL

MUSCLE BEACH

VENICE
PAVILION

PACIFIC

AVE

MAIN ST

(VENICE BOARDWALK)

SPEEDWAY

BEACH

Pacific Ocean

S
E — W
N

Venice

4TH ST

P

1

LINCOLN BLVD

ROSE AVE

MARINE

NAVY

NEILSON

THE PROMENADE

34

TO
SANTA MONICA
PIER

ALSO SEE MAPS ON
PAGES 46 • 80 • 83 • 91

HIKE 35
VENICE BEACH

the canals, connecting all the walkways. Choose your own path. The Grand Canal continues south across Washington Boulevard for 1 mile to the Marina Del Rey Harbor Channel (Hike 37).

One block west of the Grand Canal is Venice Beach and the Venice Boardwalk. The boardwalk parallels the ocean front from Washington Boulevard for 2.5 miles north to the Santa Monica Pier (Hike 35).

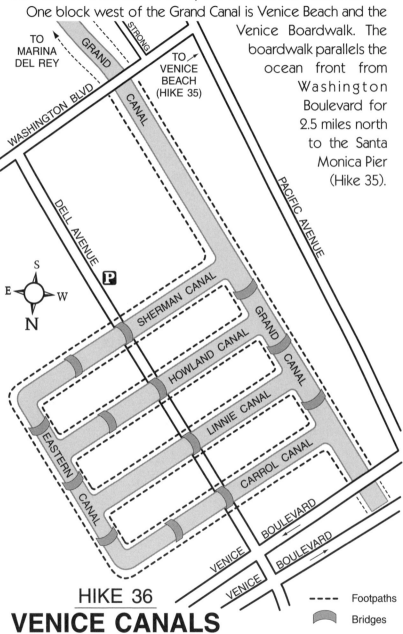

HIKE 36
VENICE CANALS

---- Footpaths

Bridges

Hike 37
Ballona Lagoon Marine Preserve
GRAND CANAL TO MARINA DEL REY HARBOR CHANNEL

Hiking distance: 2.4 mile loop
Hiking time: 1.5 hours
Elevation gain: Level
Maps: U.S.G.S. Venice

map
next page

Summary of hike: The Ballona Lagoon Marine Preserve is a 16.3-acre natural saltwater estuary between Hurricane Street (south of Washington Boulevard) and the Marina Del Rey Harbor Channel, one block inland from Venice Beach. The ocean-fed lagoon connects to Grand Canal, the main channel of the Venice Canals (Hike 36). Ballona Lagoon was originally part of the once-extensive 1,700-acre Ballona Creek wetlands, extending from Playa Del Rey to Santa Monica. The lagoon was cut off from the wetlands with the development of Marina Del Rey. The lagoon is on the 2,000-mile migratory route for birds between Alaska and Latin America, known as the Pacific Flyway. The preserve is a protected habitat for hundreds of birds, native plants, animals, and marine life. It is one of the last tidal wetlands in southern California, with high and low tides twice daily.

Driving directions: The Ballona Lagoon Marine Preserve is located between Washington Boulevard and the north side of the Marina Del Rey Harbor Channel, one block east of Pacific Avenue in Venice. From the 405 (San Diego) Freeway, take the Washington Boulevard exit, and drive 3.5 miles west towards the ocean. The trail can be accessed from several locations. This hike begins on the 300 block of Washington Boulevard. Park alongside the street or on the side streets where a parking space is available. At the west end of Washington Boulevard, 2 blocks past the lagoon, is an oceanfront parking lot for a fee.

Hiking directions: The trailhead begins on the 300 block of Washington Boulevard, just east of Strong Drive. Head south along the east bank of the Grand Canal on the narrow footpath.

Under a canopy of lush foliage, the natural path changes to a paved path between the canal and homes. At 0.4 miles, near the end of the path, curve left to Via Dolce. Cross over the wetlands on the bridge to the right. Take the rail-fenced walkway to the right, and enter the Ballona Lagoon Marine Preserve. Continue southeast through the preserve. Pass a cement bridge over the lagoon that leads to Pacific Avenue by Lighthouse Street. At the far south end of the path, just before Via Marina by the harbor channel, a boardwalk leads to an observation deck with interpretive panels about the preserve. Across Via Marina is Austin Park, a narrow, landscaped park fronting the north edge of the Marina Del Rey Harbor Channel that is a great place to view boats entering and leaving the marina. Continue to the right along the sidewalk on the west side of the street to Topsail Street. Cross the street to the dirt path along the lagoon, passing the Lighthouse Street Bridge, to Jib Street. Curve right, leaving Pacific Avenue while staying close to the lagoon. A paved path follows the west bank of Grand Canal and returns to Washington Boulevard, parallel to Strong Drive.

Hike 38
Del Rey Lagoon and Ballona Creek

Hiking distance: 2.8 miles round trip
Hiking time: 1.5 hours
Elevation gain: Level
Maps: U.S.G.S. Venice

map next page

Summary of hike: The Del Rey Lagoon in Playa Del Rey, near the Marina Del Rey Harbor Channel, is tucked between the north end of Dockweiler Beach and Ballona Creek. The 13-acre lagoon is surrounded by a grassy park with geese and ducks. It is a remnant of the original 1,700-acre Ballona Creek wetlands, stretching from Playa Del Rey to Santa Monica. Ballona Creek borders the south edge of the harbor channel and heads 9 miles inland through Culver City to the north side of the Santa Monica Freeway. This hike begins at Del Rey Lagoon and follows

Ballona Creek seaward to the mouth of the harbor and inland along the creek.

Driving directions: From the south side of Marina Del Rey at the intersection of Lincoln Boulevard and Culver Boulevard in Marina Del Rey, head 1.5 miles southwest on Culver Boulevard (towards the ocean) to Vista Del Mar at a traffic light. Stay to the right on Culver Boulevard 2 blocks to Pacific Avenue. Turn right and drive 0.4 miles to the vehicle-restricted bridge at 62nd Avenue. Park along the road where a space is available.

From the 405 (San Diego) Freeway in Culver City, take the Culver Boulevard exit and head 2.25 miles southwest (towards the ocean) to Lincoln Boulevard. Proceed with the directions above.

Hiking directions: Walk into Del Rey Lagoon Park, and stroll through the grassy park along the lagoon. Return to Pacific Avenue and head north. Cross the vehicle-restricted bridge over Ballona Creek to the walking and biking path on the levee separating Ballona Creek from the Marina Del Rey Harbor Channel. The left fork follows the paved, built-on-boulders path between the two waterways. The path leads beyond the shoreline to the end of the harbor channel, a great spot for observing boats coming in and out of the harbor. Use caution and good judgment if venturing west across the cemented boulders along the last 100 yards. Return and follow the levee inland. At a half mile past the bridge, the harbor channel curves north, away from Ballona Creek and the hiking/biking path. Continue along the paved path, or take the dirt trail to the north of the paved trail. A short distance ahead, a path curves left to Fisherman's Village, a tourist area resembling a New England sea-port town with shops, galleries, and boat docks. This is the turnaround spot.

To hike further, continue on the main trail along Ballona Creek, reaching the Lincoln Boulevard underpass 0.8 miles ahead.

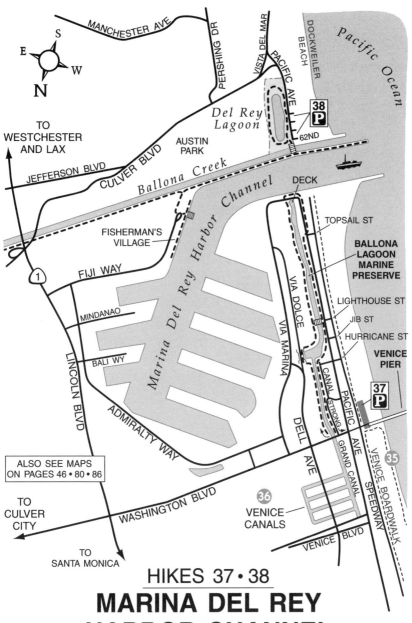

MANCHESTER AVE

PERSHING DR

VISTA DEL MAR

PACIFIC AVE

DOCKWEILER BEACH

Pacific Ocean

E S
N
W

Del Rey Lagoon

38 P

62ND

TO
WESTCHESTER
AND LAX

AUSTIN
PARK

CULVER BLVD

JEFFERSON BLVD

Ballona Creek

DECK

Marina Del Rey Harbor Channel

TOPSAIL ST

FISHERMAN'S
VILLAGE

**BALLONA
LAGOON
MARINE
PRESERVE**

FIJI WAY

1

LIGHTHOUSE ST

VIA DOLCE

JIB ST

MINDANAO

HURRICANE ST

VIA MARINA

**VENICE
PIER**

BALI WY

LINCOLN BLVD

CANAL

PACIFIC AVE

37 P

ADMIRALTY WAY

ALSO SEE MAPS
ON PAGES 46 • 80 • 86

DELL AVE

GRAND CANAL

STRONG

VENICE BOARDWALK

35

TO
CULVER
CITY

WASHINGTON BLVD

36
VENICE
CANALS

VENICE
SPEEDWAY

TO
SANTA MONICA

VENICE BLVD

HIKES 37 • 38
MARINA DEL REY
HARBOR CHANNEL
BALLONA LAGOON MARINE PRESERVE
DEL REY LAGOON • BALLONA CREEK

Hike 39
Manhattan • Hermosa • Redondo Beaches

Hiking distance: 6 miles round trip
Hiking time: 3 hours
Elevation gain: Level
Maps: U.S.G.S. Redondo Beach and Venice

Summary of hike: Manhattan, Hermosa, and Redondo Beaches are strung together along the southern end of Santa Monica Bay, known as the South Bay. They are the laid-back, quintessential southern California beaches with clean, broad, white sand beaches, popular for surfing, swimming, fishing, volleyball, and just hanging out. The three well-maintained beach communities have piers, which are surrounded by quaint shops and outdoor cafes. They have grown together, yet have retained their own distinct characters. The Strand, a paved pedestrian boardwalk lining the back end of the beaches, links the three towns and is used by walkers, joggers, and skaters. They are also connected by the South Bay Bicycle Trail, stretching 20 miles from Will Rogers State Beach (north of Santa Monica) to Redondo Beach.

Driving directions: The three beaches can be accessed from numerous routes off the San Diego Freeway, including Rosecrans Avenue, Manhattan Beach Boulevard, Artesia Boulevard, and 190th Street. This hike begins by the Manhattan Beach Pier at the end of Manhattan Beach Boulevard. From the 405 (San Diego) Freeway in Lawndale, take the Manhattan Beach Boulevard exit, and drive 2.8 miles west to downtown Manhattan Beach at Ocean Drive. Park in an available metered parking space.

Hiking directions: Walk out on the 900-foot Manhattan Beach Pier, and view the coastline from offshore. At the rounded end of the pier is a small marine lab and aquarium. Return to The Strand on the low bluffs atop the seawall and head south, passing numerous pedestrian-only walking streets that connect the residential streets to The Strand. Below are the biking trail, volleyball courts, sandy beach, and the ocean. In less than a half mile, cross into Hermosa Beach. Continue past beachfront homes and apartments to the 900-foot-long Hermosa Beach Pier at the foot of Pier Avenue. Pier Avenue is lined with outdoor restaurants and interesting shops. Continue south to King Harbor at 2.3 miles, where the beach ends. Walk inland to Harbor Drive at Herondo Street. Follow the sidewalk to the right on Harbor Drive, passing King Harbor, to the end of the road at a parking structure. Descend to the right to the walking path, and meander through horseshoe-shaped Redondo Beach Pier amid shops and restaurants. At the south end of the pier, the path leads into Veterans Park, our turnaround spot. Return by retracing your steps.

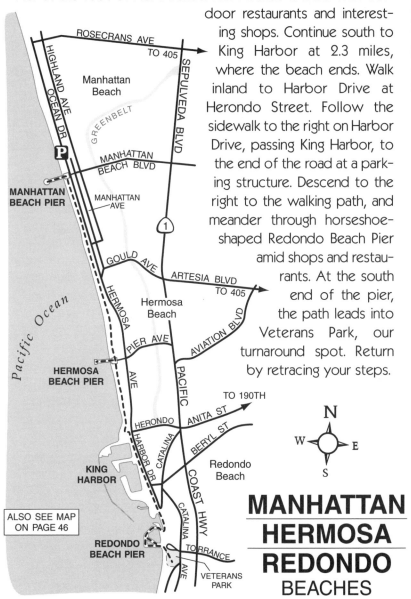

MANHATTAN
HERMOSA
REDONDO
BEACHES

Hike 40
Malaga Cove and Flat Rock Point

Hiking distance: 4 miles round trip
Hiking time: 2 hours
Elevation gain: 300 feet
Maps: U.S.G.S. Redondo Beach

Summary of hike: Malaga Cove and Flat Rock Point are at the north end of the Palos Verdes Peninsula. Malaga Canyon, formed by a major water drainage, slices through the northern slopes of the peninsula and empties into the ocean at Malaga Cove. Flat Rock Point borders the north end of Bluff Cove under soaring 300-foot cliffs. The point has some of the best tidepools in the area. This hike begins on sandy Torrance County Beach and quickly reaches the rocky tidepools and near-vertical cliffs at Malaga Cove. The trail continues along the rugged, rocky shoreline along the base of the eroded cliffs to Flat Rock Point.

Driving directions: From the Pacific Coast Highway (Highway 1) at the south end of Redondo Beach, turn south on Palos Verdes Boulevard. Drive 1.1 miles to Paseo De La Playa and turn right. Continue 0.7 miles to Torrance County Beach. Park in the lot on the left. A parking fee is required seasonally.

Hiking directions: Take the ramp down from the bluffs to the sandy beach. Head south (left), strolling on the sand towards the Palos Verdes cliffs. The views extend out to Palos Verdes Point (Hike 41). At 0.7 miles, the sand gives way to rock at the foot of the cliffs. Curve west and follow the wide walking path into Malaga Cove. Just before reaching the Palos Verdes Beach Club, a paved access path—the return route—follows stream-fed Malaga Canyon up an easy grade to the bluffs at Via Corta and Paseo Del Mar. Continue along the shoreline beneath the steep cliffs on the rounded shoreline rocks, passing Malaga Cove and the beach club. The shoreline reaches Flat Rock Point and the tidepools at 1.7 miles. From the point, cross over the rocky ridge into Bluff Cove. Curve into the crescent-shaped cove to an access trail. Hike 41 continues along the shoreline.

To return, ascend the cliffs on the wide, easy path for a quarter mile to the bluffs on Paseo Del Mar. Follow Paseo Del Mar to the left a half mile to Via Arroyo. Walk through the intersection into the parking lot on Via Arroyo, on the ocean side of Malaga Cove School. Pick up the paved Malaga Canyon Trail on the left, and descend through the canyon to the ocean, completing the loop. Return to Torrance Beach on the right.

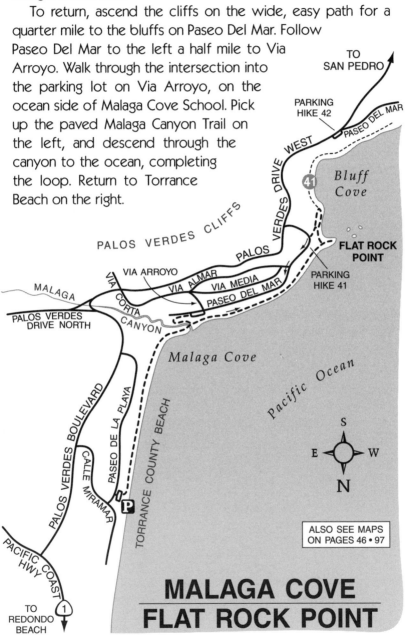

LOS ANGELES COUNTY

TO SAN PEDRO

PARKING HIKE 42

PASEO DEL MAR

Bluff Cove

FLAT ROCK POINT

VERDES DRIVE WEST

PALOS VERDES CLIFFS

PALOS

VIA ARROYO

VIA CORTA

VIA ALMAR

VIA MEDIA

PASEO DEL MAR

PARKING HIKE 41

MALAGA

PALOS VERDES DRIVE NORTH

CANYON

Malaga Cove

Pacific Ocean

PALOS VERDES BOULEVARD

CALLE MIRAMAR

PASEO DE LA PLAYA

TORRANCE COUNTY BEACH

S
E W
N

ALSO SEE MAPS ON PAGES 46 • 97

PACIFIC COAST HWY

TO REDONDO BEACH

1

MALAGA COVE
FLAT ROCK POINT

Hike 41
Bluff Cove to Lunada Bay

Hiking distance: 6 miles round trip
Hiking time: 3 hours
Elevation gain: 300 feet
Maps: U.S.G.S. Redondo Beach

Summary of hike: Bluff Cove and Lunada Bay are both crescent-shaped rocky beach pockets resting beneath sheer, terraced cliffs. They are popular with surfers and tidepoolers. The path begins at Flat Rock Point and leads down to the rocky Bluff Cove. The jagged shore, lined with cliffs, passes numerous smaller coves as it winds to horseshoe-shaped Lunada Bay. This bay is bounded by Palos Verdes Point (also known as Rocky Point) and Resort Point. In 1961, a Greek freighter named *Dominator*, en route from Vancouver, Canada, to the Los Angeles Harbor, ran aground in thick fog just north of Rocky Point. Watch for the rusted remnants of the abandoned ship.

Driving directions: From the Pacific Coast Highway (Highway 1) at the south end of Redondo Beach, turn south on Palos Verdes Boulevard. (See map on page 95.) Drive 1.5 miles and curve to the right onto Palos Verdes Drive West to the first stop sign. Turn right on Via Corta. Drive 0.4 miles and turn right on Via Arroyo. Drive one block to Paseo Del Mar. Turn left and continue 0.5 miles to a distinct path on a left bend in the road. Surfers' vehicles are often parked along this bend.

Hiking directions: Take the wide path down the cliffs on an easy, tapered grade overlooking the rock formations at Flat Rock Point. At the north end of Bluff Cove, a steep side path descends to the tidepools at Flat Rock Point. The main trail curves left into the rocky beach at crescent-shaped Bluff Cove. Slowly follow the shoreline southwest, walking over the eroded boulders under the 300-foot bluffs. As you approach Rocky Point, watch for scattered remains of the *Dominator*. Follow the point into Lunada Bay. As you circle the bay, watch for a steep path ascending the cliffs, just before Agua Amarga Canyon. Carefully climb up the eroded cliffs to the grassy open space atop the bluffs. If you prefer to continue hiking along the shoreline, follow Lunada Bay around Resort Point into a small pocket cove. Another precipitous trail ascends the cliffs to the open space on the bluffs. Return northbound along the bluffs, following Paseo Del Mar and Palos Verdes Drive .

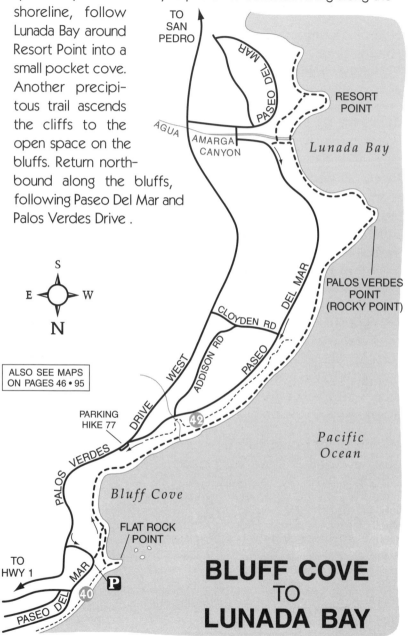

TO
SAN
PEDRO

PASEO DEL MAR

RESORT
POINT

AGUA

AMARGA
CANYON

Lunada Bay

S

E — W

N

PALOS VERDES
POINT
(ROCKY POINT)

DEL MAR

CLOYDEN RD

PASEO

ADDISON RD

WEST

ALSO SEE MAPS
ON PAGES 46 • 95

DRIVE

PARKING
HIKE 77

42

PALOS VERDES

*Pacific
Ocean*

Bluff Cove

FLAT ROCK
POINT

TO
HWY 1

DEL MAR

P

40

PASEO DEL MAR

BLUFF COVE
TO
LUNADA BAY

Hike 42
Paseo Del Mar Bluffs
PALOS VERDES ESTATES SHORELINE PRESERVE

Hiking distance: 1.3 miles round trip
Hiking time: 45 minutes
Elevation gain: Level
Maps: U.S.G.S. Redondo Beach

Summary of hike: The Palos Verdes Estates Shoreline Preserve is a 130-acre undeveloped stretch of land running 4.5 miles along the coast. The city-owned preserve includes scalloped blufftop parklands, footpaths that lead from the overlooks to the rocky shore, plus the adjacent submerged offshore land. This hike follows the grassy oceanfront bluffs high above Bluff Cove, parallel to Paseo Del Mar. From the cliff's edge are incredible views of Bluff Cove, Catalina Island, the Channel Islands, and the beach cities along Santa Monica Bay to Point Dume. It is also a great area to view migrating whales.

Driving directions: From the Pacific Coast Highway (Highway 1) at the south end of Redondo Beach, turn south on Palos Verdes Boulevard. (See map on page 95.) Drive 1.5 miles and curve to the right onto Palos Verdes Drive West to the first stop sign at Via Corta. Continue straight ahead for 1.7 miles to a parking lot on the right, just before the Paseo Del Mar turnoff.

Hiking directions: Take the grassy blufftop path from the south end of Bluff Cove. The parkland parallels the crenulated cliffs bordered by Paseo Del Mar. The level, cliff-top trail leaves the edge of the cliffs and curves inland, looping around a stream-carved gorge before returning to the cliffs. The meandering path ends at a row of palm trees adjacent to an oceanfront residence across from Cloyden Road. Return along the same route.

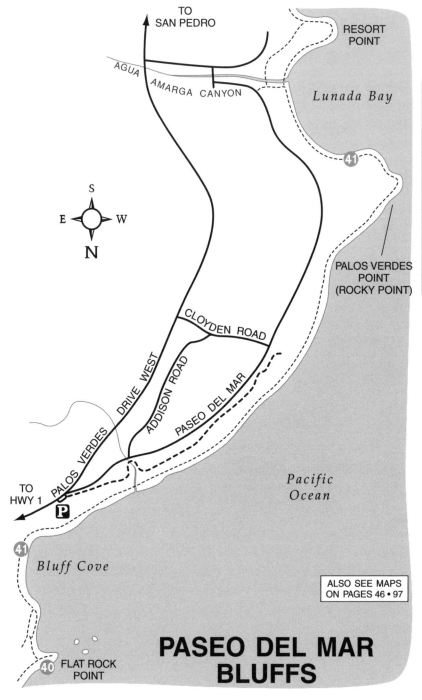

TO
SAN PEDRO

RESORT
POINT

AGUA

AMARGA CANYON

Lunada Bay

LOS ANGELES COUNTY

S

E — W

N

41

PALOS VERDES
POINT
(ROCKY POINT)

CLOYDEN ROAD

PALOS VERDES DRIVE WEST

ADDISON ROAD

PASEO DEL MAR

Pacific Ocean

TO
HWY 1

P

41

Bluff Cove

ALSO SEE MAPS
ON PAGES 46 • 97

40 FLAT ROCK
POINT

PASEO DEL MAR
BLUFFS

Hike 43
Point Vicente Fishing Access Trail to
Point Vicente and Long Point

Hiking distance: 1.5 miles round trip
Hiking time: 1 hour
Elevation gain: 140 feet
Maps: U.S.G.S. Redondo Beach

Summary of hike: Point Vicente is situated on the southwest point of the Palos Verdes Peninsula. Perched on the cliffs, high above the shore, is the historic 67-foot Point Vicente Lighthouse, built in 1926. From the 140-foot scalloped bluffs are vistas of the lighthouse, Santa Catalina Island, and Long Point, the former site of Marineland on the southeast end of the bay. This is a premier spot for observing the migrating gray whales from mid-December through March. The Point Vicente Fishing Access Trail descends the eroding cliffs to the rounded cobblestone beach with tidepools full of marine life beneath Point Vicente and Long Point. The crescent-shaped bay with large offshore rocks is a popular site for scuba divers, surfers, and anglers.

Driving directions: From the Pacific Coast Highway (Highway 1) at the south end of Torrance, take Hawthorne Boulevard south 7.3 miles to its terminus at the coast. Turn left on Palos Verdes Drive South, and drive 0.8 miles to the posted fishing access. Park in the lot on the right.

Hiking directions: Walk to the west (upper) end of the parking lot. Take the well-defined dirt path, just beyond the restrooms. Descend the cliffs on an easy grade towards the prominent Point Vicente Lighthouse. Halfway down the slope, switchback left, dropping down to the rocky cobblestone shoreline. The beach pocket is bordered on the west by steep cliffs and a natural rock jetty. On the south end, the beach ends near Long Point, where the cliffs drop 100 feet into the sea near the offshore rock outcroppings.

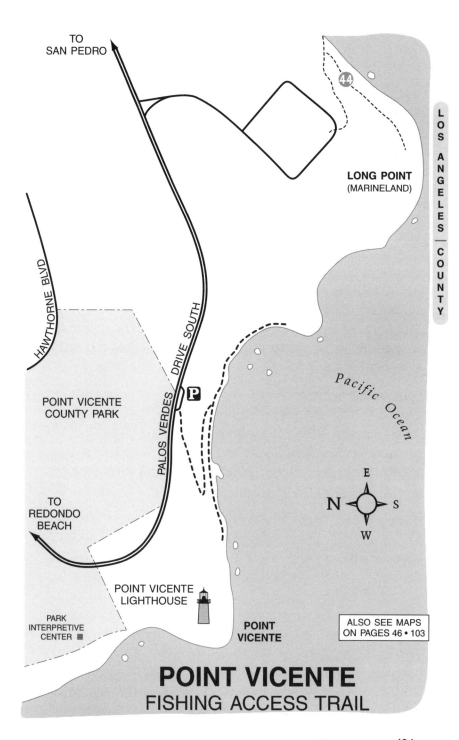

TO
SAN PEDRO

44

LONG POINT
(MARINELAND)

LOS ANGELES COUNTY

HAWTHORNE BLVD

PALOS VERDES DRIVE SOUTH

P

POINT VICENTE
COUNTY PARK

Pacific Ocean

TO
REDONDO
BEACH

E
N — S
W

POINT VICENTE
LIGHTHOUSE

POINT
VICENTE

PARK
INTERPRETIVE
CENTER

ALSO SEE MAPS
ON PAGES 46 • 103

POINT VICENTE
FISHING ACCESS TRAIL

Hike 44
Long Point
(MARINELAND)

Hiking distance: 1 mile round trip
Hiking time: 45 minutes
Elevation gain: 100 feet
Maps: U.S.G.S. Redondo Beach

Summary of hike: Long Point extends seaward at the south-west point of the Palos Verdes Peninsula. Marineland, a defunct 108-acre marine amusement park, was situated on the bluffs atop Long Point from 1954 to 1987. It closed due to its remote-ness and competition from modern aquatic parks and aquari-ums. Beach access is still permitted from the enormous Marineland parking lot atop the 100-foot bluffs. The trail descends the eroded cliffs to an isolated beach pocket at the base of the vertical cliffs. It is a popular snorkeling and scuba diving area.

Driving directions: From the Pacific Coast Highway (Highway 1) at the south end of Torrance, take Hawthorne Boulevard south 7.3 miles to its terminus at the coast. Turn left on Palos Verdes Drive South, and drive 1.3 miles to the Long Point turnoff, the old entrance to Marineland. Turn right and drive 0.4 miles to the far southwest corner of the parking lot.

Hiking directions: Take the partially paved road/trail past the vehicle barrier. Descend to the east overlooking Abalone Cove and Portuguese Point (Hike 45). Halfway down the descent is a large flat area and trail split. The road continues straight ahead to the sheer, eroding cliffs and rocky beach pocket. Watch for a narrow, intermittent waterfall dropping 60 feet off the cliffs. After exploring the tidepools and rock for-mations at the beach, return to the trail split. Bear left, leaving the road, and take the dirt path along the edge of the 100-foot bluffs. Slowly descend to the tip of rocky Long Point, where the pelicans line the ridge. Return along the same route.

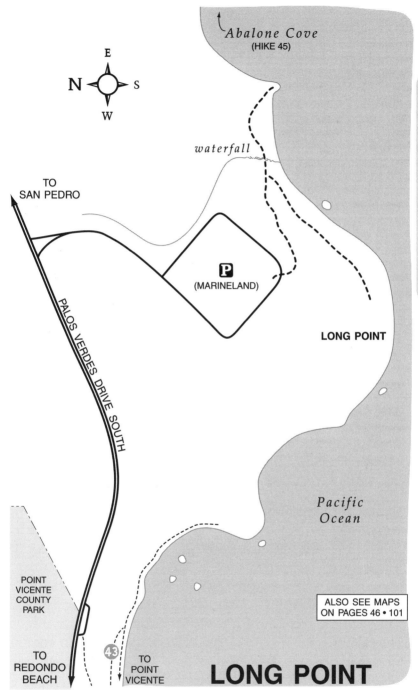

Abalone Cove
(HIKE 45)

N E S W

TO
SAN PEDRO

waterfall

P
(MARINELAND)

PALOS VERDES DRIVE SOUTH

L O S   A N G E L E S   C O U N T Y

LONG POINT

Pacific Ocean

POINT
VICENTE
COUNTY
PARK

ALSO SEE MAPS
ON PAGES 46 • 101

TO
REDONDO
BEACH

43

TO
POINT
VICENTE

LONG POINT

Hike 45
Abalone Cove and Portuguese Point
5970 Palos Verdes Drive South

Hiking distance: 2 miles round trip
Hiking time: 1 hour
Elevation gain: 150 feet
Maps: U.S.G.S. Redondo Beach and San Pedro

Summary of hike: Abalone Cove Shoreline Park and Ecological Preserve, on the southern shoreline of the Palos Verdes Peninsula, is a federal reserve where grassy 180-foot bluffs easily access the rocky shoreline. The 80-acre preserve extends from Abalone Cove to Portuguese Point and Sacred Cove (also known as Smugglers Cove). Sacred Cove is bordered by tidepools at both points. From Portuguese Point are magnificent views of Abalone Cove, Long Point (Hike 44), Sacred Cove, Inspiration Point, White Point (Hike 46), Point Fermin, and Catalina Island. The oceanfront park sits at the foot of the unstable and actively slipping Portuguese Bend landslide area.

Driving directions: From the Pacific Coast Highway (Highway 1) at the south end of Torrance, take Hawthorne Boulevard south 7.3 miles to its terminus at the coast. Turn left on Palos Verdes Drive South, and drive 2.2 miles to the posted Abalone Cove Shoreline Park entrance. Turn right and park in the lot. A parking fee is required.

Hiking directions: From the east end of the parking lot, cross the grassy picnic area onto a wide gravel path. Continue to a vehicle-restricted road. Bear left and wind up the hillside on the vehicle-restricted road to Palos Verdes Drive. Bear to the left on the narrow path, parallel to the highway, for 0.2 miles to the Portuguese Point access. Walk up the curving, gated road to the north edge of the peninsula and a trail split. First, take the left fork out to Portuguese Point, which stays atop the peninsula and loops around the perimeter. After enjoying the awesome coastal views from the point, return to the trail split Take the left fork down to the beach and tide-pools near an old rock enclosure. The trail to the left leads to the base of the cliffs at Portuguese Point. To return, follow the shoreline trail back along Abalone Cove for 0.4 miles to Upper Beach, a raised, man-made sandy beach and lifeguard station just above the rocky shore. Curve right and take the old paved road to a trail junction. The footpath to the left ascends the cliffs through the dense brush, back to the parking lot.

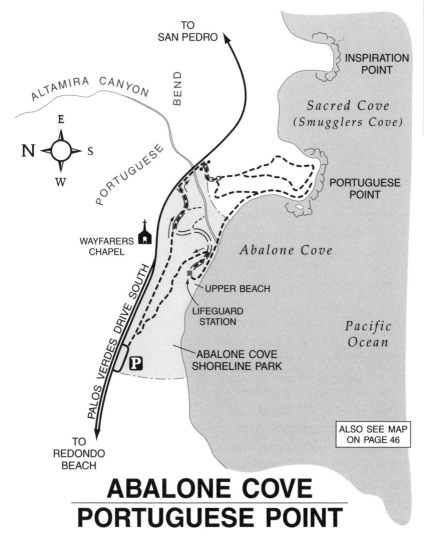

ABALONE COVE
PORTUGUESE POINT

Hike 46
White Point and Point Fermin Park

Hiking distance: 4 miles round trip
Hiking time: 2 hours
Elevation gain: 100 feet
Maps: U.S.G.S. San Pedro

Summary of hike: White Point in San Pedro was home to the Royal Palms Hotel, a booming spa resort with hot sulphur pools predating the 1920s. Falling victim to storms, pounding surf, and an earthquake in 1933, all that remain are majestic palms, garden terraces, and remnants of the concrete foundation. To the east of the point is White Point Beach, a rocky cove with tidepools below the sedimentary cliffs. Point Fermin Park, located at the southernmost point in Los Angeles County, sits atop grassy tree-shaded bluffs jutting prominently out to sea. The scenic 37-acre park has flower gardens, mature fig trees, and curving pathways that lead from the bluffs to the rocky shoreline. Point Fermin Lighthouse is an historic Victorian structure that sits on the edge of the vertical cliffs. It was built in 1874 with lumber and bricks shipped around Cape Horn. The lighthouse was in use for nearly a century.

Driving directions: From the intersection of Western Avenue and 25th Street in San Pedro, drive 0.5 miles south to the end of Western Avenue at the coastline. Curve left onto South Paseo Del Mar, and drive 0.1 miles to the White Point Park parking lot on the right. Park in the lot for a fee or alongside the road for free.

Hiking directions: Descend the cliffs on the dirt path or walk west down the paved road to Royal Palms Beach Park. Head east and follow the coastline around White Point, crossing over small boulders and slabs of rock. Stroll along the rocky shore of White Point Beach below the ruins of the Royal Palms Hotel. Continue following the shoreline past a group of old homes at the base of the sheer 120-foot cliffs. At 1.2 miles, take the distinct path on the left, and head up the cliffs to the west. Half way up, the path becomes paved. Wind through a palm tree grove and to the top of the bluffs across from Barbara Street, at the west end of Point Fermin Park. Continue east for one mile through the narrow tree-shaded park along the edge of the grassy bluffs to Point Fermin and the lighthouse. This is our turn-around spot. Return along the same path, or follow South Paseo Del Mar back to the trail-head. To extend the hike, continue through Sunken City (Hike 47).

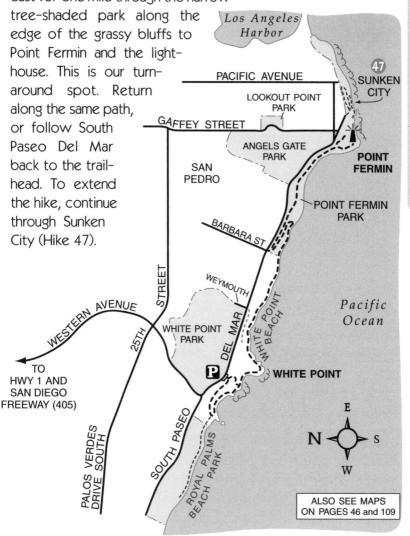

WHITE POINT
POINT FERMIN PARK

Hike 47
Sunken City

Hiking distance: 0.8 miles round trip
Hiking time: 1 hour
Elevation gain: 100 feet
Maps: U.S.G.S. San Pedro

Summary of hike: Sunken City sits on six acres of slipping, eroding, and sinking land adjacent to Point Fermin Park. The "city," at the southernmost point in Los Angeles County, was once a neighborhood of exclusive homes. Waves undercut the base of the sandstone and shale cliffs, which began slumping and sliding in 1929 and again in the early 1940s. It is now a jumble of rolling land with palm trees, isolated slabs of the old road, tilting sidewalks, streetcar tracks, remnants of house foundations, and chimneys above the surf-swept rocky seashore. Several meandering paths weave through the bluffs. Exploring this surreal landscape is like entering the "twilight zone." The Point Fermin Marine Life Refuge follows a half-mile stretch of the coastline below. A few trails drop down the dramatic cliffs to the rocky shoreline and tidal pools.

Driving directions: From the south end of the Harbor Freeway (Interstate 110) in San Pedro, take the Gaffey Street exit. Continue south to the end of Gaffey Street on the ocean-front bluffs at South Paseo Del Mar. Park straight ahead in the Point Fermin Park parking lot.

Hiking directions: At the east (left) end of the parking area, walk around the 3-foot concrete boundary used as a warning barrier. Step around the chainlink fence, and bear left to the edge of the bluffs and a junction. The right fork descends the sheer eroded cliffs to the rocky shoreline and bountiful tidepools. For now, stay to the left, choosing one of several paths that meander through the rolling maze of the old neighborhood. After exploring the tangled terrain and shoreline, visit the historic Point Fermin Lighthouse, built in 1874.

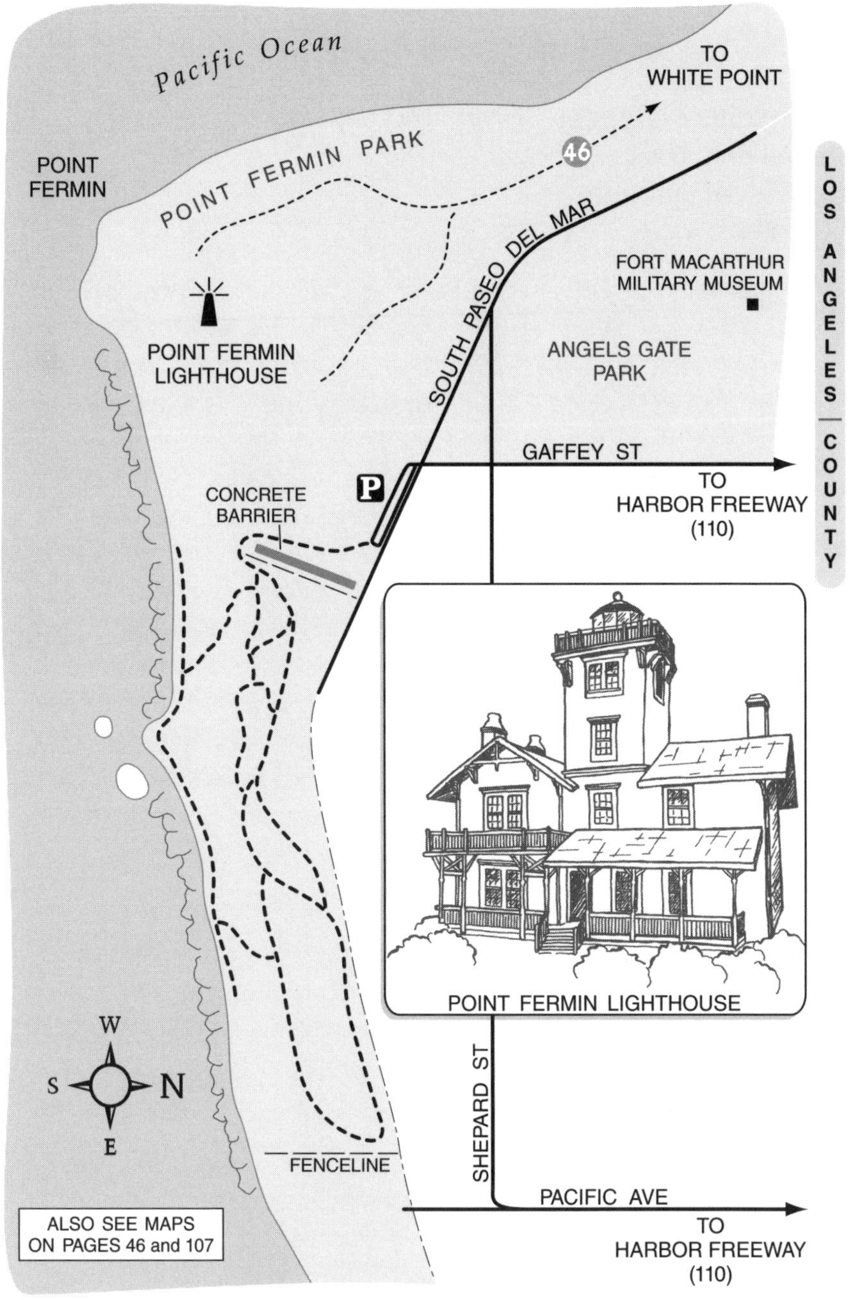

Pacific Ocean

TO
WHITE POINT

POINT
FERMIN

POINT FERMIN PARK

46

SOUTH PASEO DEL MAR

FORT MACARTHUR
MILITARY MUSEUM

POINT FERMIN
LIGHTHOUSE

ANGELS GATE
PARK

GAFFEY ST

TO
HARBOR FREEWAY
(110)

CONCRETE
BARRIER

P

POINT FERMIN LIGHTHOUSE

W

S — N

E

SHEPARD ST

FENCELINE

PACIFIC AVE

TO
HARBOR FREEWAY
(110)

ALSO SEE MAPS
ON PAGES 46 and 107

LOS ANGELES | COUNTY

SUNKEN CITY

Hike 48
Long Beach Oceanfront Trail

Hiking distance: 7 miles round trip
Hiking time: 3.5 hours
Elevation gain: Level
Maps: U.S.G.S. Long Beach

Summary of hike: Long Beach is the southernmost coastal city in Los Angeles County. Long Beach City Beach extends 4 miles from the Long Beach Harbor to the Alamitos Peninsula and San Gabriel River on the Orange County line. This hike begins at the mouth of the Los Angeles River in Queensway Bay by Shoreline Village, a tourist attraction with shops and restaurants. The path follows the coastline along Long Beach City Beach and Bluff Park to Belmont Pier. Bluff Park is an elevated grassy park above the wide, sandy beach, overlooking San Pedro Bay. Bluff Park backs the beach and runs parallel to Ocean Boulevard. Bisecting Long Beach City Beach is Belmont Pier, a 1,600-foot T-shaped pier. The pier was built in 1968 at the foot of 39th Place in Belmont Shore, a charming seaside community filled with shops and restaurants. Offshore from the beach are four artificial tropical islands with postcard-perfect fronts. They are actually landscaped oil drilling platforms.

Driving directions: From the 405 (San Diego) Freeway in Long Beach, take 710 (Long Beach Freeway) south to its end. Follow the Downtown Long Beach/Aquarium signs onto Shoreline Drive. Turn right and curve into the huge Long Beach Marina parking lot, and park near Shoreline Village. A parking fee is required.

Hiking directions: Follow the paved walking and biking path along the Downtown Shoreline Marina to Shoreline Village. Curve left along the narrow, palm-lined breakwater in Queensway Bay. Pass the Queen Mary, an 81,000-ton luxury liner built in 1934 and retired after more than a thousand transatlantic voyages. Continue past several short fishing and overlook piers for a half mile to the breakwater's end, across from Island Grissom. Return to Shoreline Village and continue 0.5 miles east, passing the marina boat slips. The path curves away from the small marina to the back end of wide, sandy Long Beach City Beach. Continue east, curving past the historic life-guard station built in 1938, to a parking lot where Junipero Avenue winds down the bluffs to the shoreline parking lot. Climb up the stairs to grassy Bluff Park, just west of Lindero Avenue. Follow the tree-filled park 0.8 miles on the 40-foot bluffs to Loma Avenue. Descend the stairway to the beach and follow the coastline, rising to the base of Belmont Pier off of 39th Place in Belmont Shore. This is the turnaround spot. To continue hiking, the oceanfront trail continues to Alamitos Peninsula, 2 miles further.

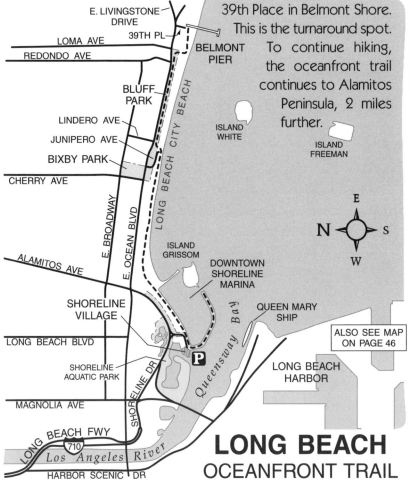

LONG BEACH
OCEANFRONT TRAIL

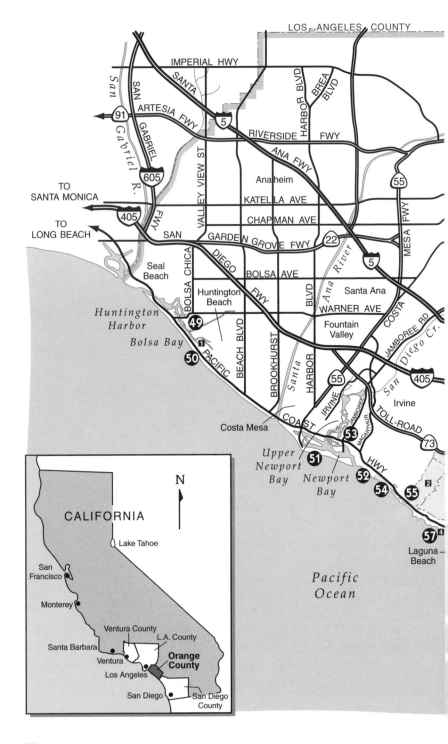

LOS ANGELES COUNTY

IMPERIAL HWY

San Gabriel R.

SANTA FWY

SAN GABRIEL FWY

91

ARTESIA FWY

TO SANTA MONICA

TO LONG BEACH

605

405

SAN

VALLEY VIEW ST

HARBOR BLVD

BREA BLVD

5

RIVERSIDE FWY

ANA FWY

Anaheim

KATELLA AVE

CHAPMAN AVE

GARDEN GROVE FWY

22

55

MESA FWY

5

Seal Beach

BOLSA CHICA

SAN DIEGO FWY

BOLSA AVE

Huntington Beach

Santa Ana

BLVD

WARNER AVE

Huntington Harbor

Bolsa Bay

49

1

50

PACIFIC

BEACH BLVD

BROOKHURST

Fountain Valley

Santa Ana River

HARBOR

Ana River

55

COSTA

JAMBOREE RD

San Diego Cr.

405

Irvine

COAST

IRVINE

JAMBOREE

TOLL-ROAD

73

Costa Mesa

MACARTHUR

53

Upper Newport Bay

51

Newport Bay

HWY

52

54

55

2

57 4

Laguna Beach

Pacific Ocean

N

CALIFORNIA

Lake Tahoe

San Francisco

Monterey

Ventura County

L.A. County

Santa Barbara

Ventura

Orange County

Los Angeles

San Diego

San Diego County

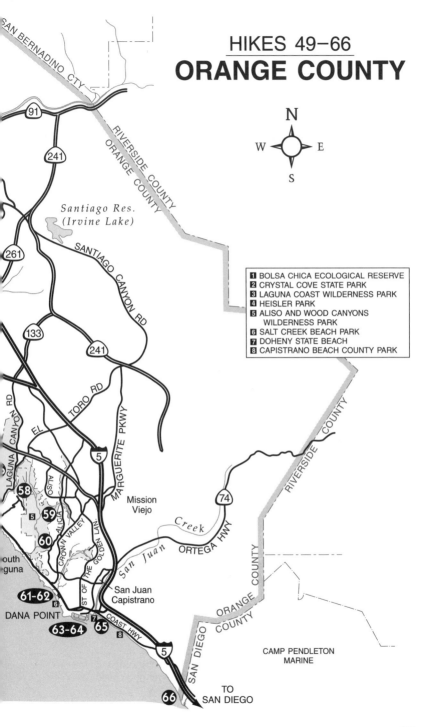

1 BOLSA CHICA ECOLOGICAL RESERVE
2 CRYSTAL COVE STATE PARK
3 LAGUNA COAST WILDERNESS PARK
4 HEISLER PARK
5 ALISO AND WOOD CANYONS
  WILDERNESS PARK
6 SALT CREEK BEACH PARK
7 DOHENY STATE BEACH
8 CAPISTRANO BEACH COUNTY PARK

ORANGE COUNTY

Hike 49
Bolsa Chica Ecological Reserve

Hiking distance: 3 mile loop
Hiking time: 1.5 hours
Elevation gain: 20 feet
Maps: U.S.G.S. Seal Beach

Summary of hike: The Bolsa Chica tidal basin encompasses 1,300 wetland acres and 300 mesa acres between Seal Beach and Huntington Beach, adjacent to Bolsa Chica State Beach. The Bolsa Chica Ecological Reserve is a 557-acre protected wildlife habitat within the Bolsa Bay wetlands. The preserve, established in 1973, has inter-tidal mudflats, salt flats, salt marsh communities, ponds, grasslands, lowland dunes, two bird nesting islands, and flood control channels. The reserve is on the Pacific Flyway, a 2,000-mile migratory bird route between Alaska and Latin America. This hike begins near the Outer Bay and loops around the slough, passing interpretive panels and overlooks with benches for wildlife viewing.

Driving directions: From the 405 (San Diego) Freeway in Fountain Valley, take the Warner Avenue West exit. Drive 5.5 miles west to the well-signed trailhead parking lot and interpretive center on the left. The parking lot is located after crossing the bridge over the Bolsa Bay Channel and before the Pacific Coast Highway.

The southern trailhead access is located on the Pacific Coast Highway, 1.4 miles south of Warner Avenue.

Hiking directions: From the interpretive center, walk east, past the trailhead kiosks, to the west edge of the Bolsa Bay tidal waters. Bear left and cross the Warner Avenue Bridge on the shoulder of the road. Pick up the trail to the right. Follow the 15-foot high mesa terrace on the west edge of the grassy open expanse on the east bank of the water channel. Just shy of a palm tree grove is a trail split. Stay to the right, on the levee along the slough. Both paths rejoin at an overlook of the coast-

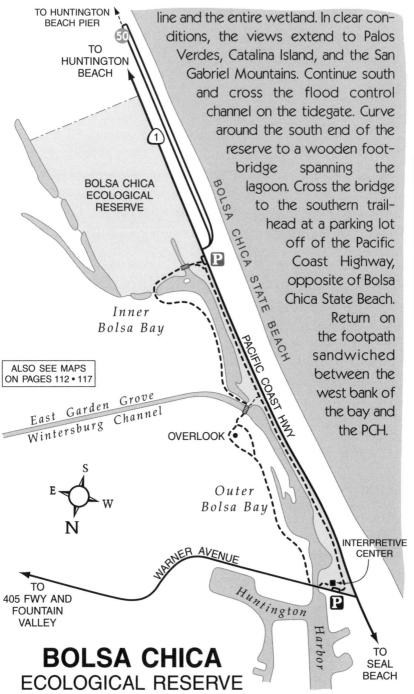

line and the entire wetland. In clear conditions, the views extend to Palos Verdes, Catalina Island, and the San Gabriel Mountains. Continue south and cross the flood control channel on the tidegate. Curve around the south end of the reserve to a wooden footbridge spanning the lagoon. Cross the bridge to the southern trailhead at a parking lot off of the Pacific Coast Highway, opposite of Bolsa Chica State Beach. Return on the footpath sandwiched between the west bank of the bay and the PCH.

TO HUNTINGTON
BEACH PIER

50

TO
HUNTINGTON
BEACH

1

BOLSA CHICA
ECOLOGICAL
RESERVE

BOLSA CHICA STATE BEACH

ORANGE COUNTY

Inner
Bolsa Bay

PACIFIC COAST HWY

ALSO SEE MAPS
ON PAGES 112 • 117

East Garden Grove
Winfersburg Channel

OVERLOOK

S
E W
N

Outer
Bolsa Bay

WARNER AVENUE

Huntington

INTERPRETIVE
CENTER

TO
405 FWY AND
FOUNTAIN
VALLEY

Harbor

TO
SEAL
BEACH

BOLSA CHICA
ECOLOGICAL RESERVE

Hike 50
Huntington Beach • Bluff Top Park
BOLSA CHICA STATE BEACH TO HUNTINGTON PIER

Hiking distance: 5.6 miles round trip
Hiking time: 3 hours
Elevation gain: 30 feet
Maps: U.S.G.S. Seal Beach

Summary of hike: Huntington City Beach is a 3.5-mile strand of wide, sandy shoreline between Bolsa Chica State Beach and Huntington State Beach. Huntington Beach, known as Surf City, is one of Orange County's most popular surfing beaches. This hike follows the 30-foot bluffs of Bluff Top Park, from the south end of Bolsa Chica State Beach to Huntington Pier. Huntington Pier is at the foot of Main Street, the busy beach hub with shops and restaurants. The 1,850-foot long pier, built in 1914, is lit with floodlights for after-dark fishing and surfing. The beach is lined with low bluffs and an 8.5-mile walking and biking path from Bolsa Chica State Beach through Huntington Beach to the Santa Ana River.

Driving directions: From the 405 (San Diego) Freeway in Fountain Valley, take the Warner Avenue West exit. Take Warner Avenue 5.6 miles west to the Pacific Coast Highway at the ocean. Turn left and drive 1.5 miles to the Bolsa Chica State Beach parking lot on the right. Turn right into the lot and curve left. Continue 0.9 miles and park at the south end of the lot.

Hiking directions: From the south end of the Bolsa Chica State Beach parking lot, head south along the low dunes on the paved walking and biking path. The path gently rises through low-growing vegetation, which stabilizes the dunes, up to Bluff Top Park. The palm-lined, grassy park sits at the top of the eroding 30-foot bluffs. Continue south along either of two parallel paths—a walking path on the west or a biking path ten feet to the east. At 2.4 miles, adjacent to 11th Street, the path drops down to the sand in front of a sloping, grassy park and the

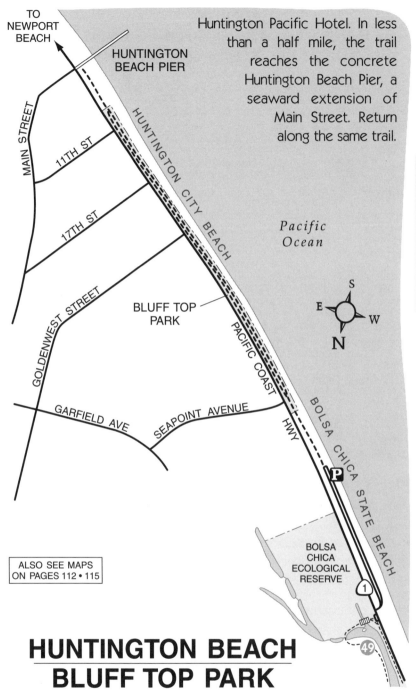

TO
NEWPORT
BEACH

HUNTINGTON
BEACH PIER

MAIN STREET

11TH ST

17TH ST

GOLDENWEST STREET

HUNTINGTON CITY BEACH

BLUFF TOP
PARK

PACIFIC COAST

GARFIELD AVE

SEAPOINT AVENUE

HWY

Huntington Pacific Hotel. In less than a half mile, the trail reaches the concrete Huntington Beach Pier, a seaward extension of Main Street. Return along the same trail.

*Pacific
Ocean*

S

E

W

N

ORANGE COUNTY

BOLSA CHICA STATE BEACH

P

BOLSA
CHICA
ECOLOGICAL
RESERVE

1

49

ALSO SEE MAPS
ON PAGES 112 • 115

HUNTINGTON BEACH
BLUFF TOP PARK

Hike 51
Newport Beach • Balboa Peninsula
NEWPORT PIER TO WEST JETTY VIEW PARK

Hiking distance: 5.6 miles round trip
Hiking time: 3 hours
Elevation gain: Level
Maps: U.S.G.S. Newport Beach
Franko's Map of Newport Harbor

Summary of hike: Newport Beach and Balboa Beach are broad, white sand beaches on Balboa Peninsula, a 4-mile long finger of land between the Newport Bay Harbor and the Pacific Ocean. Newport Beach and Newport Pier are at the west end of the peninsula. The public fishing pier, built in 1888, is the oldest pier in southern California. Balboa Beach and Balboa Pier are to the east. Adjacent to the pier is Peninsula Park, an expansive grassland with palm trees, ball fields, and picnic areas. At the peninsula's tip, by the mouth of the harbor, is West Jetty View Park and The Wedge, a popular body surfing area in the elbow of the jetty. From the park are views across the channel to the rock formations and beach coves in Corona Del Mar (Hike 52). This hike strolls along the Balboa Peninsula on the oceanfront promenade from the Newport Pier to West Jetty View Park at the mouth of the bay.

Driving directions: From the 405 (San Diego) Freeway in Costa Mesa, take the Harbor Boulevard south exit. Drive 3.2 miles to Newport Boulevard. Turn right and continue 2 miles south towards the Balboa Peninsula. Just after 23rd Street, veer right towards the signed "Beach Parking" by Newport Pier, curving right onto 22nd Street to the oceanfront parking lot.

Hiking directions: From Newport Pier, head southeast on the boardwalk. Stroll between beachfront homes and the back of the sandy beach. At just over a half mile, pass a wide, grassy park between 14th and 13th Streets, and continue to Balboa Pier at 1.8 miles. Peninsula Park stretches for two blocks from the pier to B Street. The boardwalk ends a quarter mile beyond the park, just east of E Street at 2.1 miles. Continue east on the sandy beachfront, passing paved beach accesses that cross the dunes. The beach ends at the tip of the peninsula in West Jetty View Park near the harbor channel. The palm-lined park has a paved walking path and benches. It is a great spot for observing the boats and rock outcroppings across the harbor.

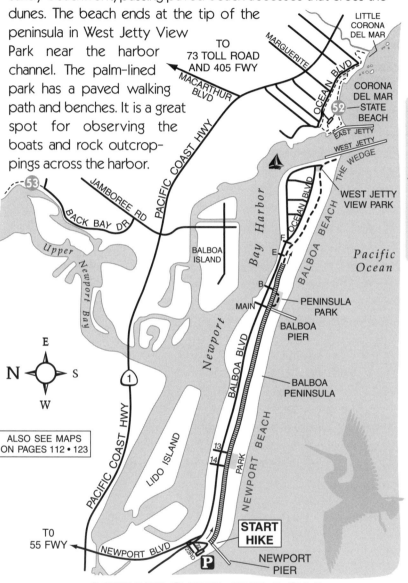

LITTLE CORONA DEL MAR

MARGUERITE

TO 73 TOLL ROAD AND 405 FWY

MACARTHUR BLVD

OCEAN BLVD

CORONA DEL MAR STATE BEACH

52

EAST JETTY

WEST JETTY

THE WEDGE

WEST JETTY VIEW PARK

OCEAN BLVD

BALBOA BEACH

Pacific Ocean

PACIFIC COAST HWY

JAMBOREE RD

BACK BAY DR

53

Upper Newport Bay

Bay Harbor

BALBOA ISLAND

Newport

F

E

B

MAIN

PENINSULA PARK

BALBOA PIER

BALBOA PENINSULA

E

N ⊕ S

W

BALBOA BLVD

(1)

NEWPORT BEACH

PARK

13

14

ALSO SEE MAPS ON PAGES 112 • 123

PACIFIC COAST HWY

LIDO ISLAND

TO 55 FWY

NEWPORT BLVD

P

START HIKE

NEWPORT PIER

NEWPORT BEACH
BALBOA PENINSULA

Hike 52
Corona Del Mar State Beach

Hiking distance: 1.5 mile loop
Hiking time: 1 hour
Elevation gain: 50 feet
Maps: U.S.G.S. Newport Beach and Laguna Beach
Franko's Map of Newport Harbor

Summary of hike: Corona Del Mar, meaning "Crown of the Sea," is a small blufftop community on the east side of Newport Harbor. It is located at the start of the scenic oceanfront cliffs that extend south to San Clemente and San Onofre. The beach, which sits at the mouth of the harbor, is a triangular wedge of land with gorgeous white sand coves beneath 80-foot bluffs. The state beach has tidepools and offshore rock formations. To the south, a stream-fed canyon drains through Little Corona Del Mar Beach, a secluded cove with lush riparian vegetation in the Robert E. Badham Marine Life Refuge. This hike begins at the east jetty of Newport Harbor and explores the beaches and marine refuges, from the palisades to the sandy beaches.

Driving directions: From the 405 (San Diego) Freeway in Irvine, take the Jamboree Road exit. Drive 1.6 miles south to Macarthur Boulevard and turn left. Continue 4 miles to the Pacific Coast Highway and turn left. Drive 0.6 miles to Marguerite Avenue and turn right. Go two blocks to Ocean Boulevard and turn right. In one block, veer left and descend to the posted beach parking. Park near the north end of the parking lot.

Hiking directions: Walk west to the jagged rock formations at the Newport Bay Harbor Channel. Explore the rocks, caves, and sandy beach pocket. To the south, a path follows the seawall along the edge of the channel to the rock jetty. To the north, atop the rock formation, a footpath leads to Lookout Point, a blufftop park that overlooks the harbor and Balboa Peninsula. From the lookout, stroll southeast along the bluffs. Parallel Ocean Boulevard to Inspiration Point, a small park at the foot of Orchid Avenue that overlooks Corona Del Mar Beach and the offshore rock formations. The walkway leading down the cliffs is our return route. For now, continue east to an overlook with a bench by Poppy Avenue. Descend on the paved path into Little Corona Del Mar Beach, a beach pocket tucked between vertical rock cliffs with tidepools and scenic offshore rocks carved by wind and pounding surf. Return to Inspiration Point on the bluffs. Descend on the walkway down the cliffs past an overlook extending off the rocky knob. Cross the sandy beach, returning to the parking lot.

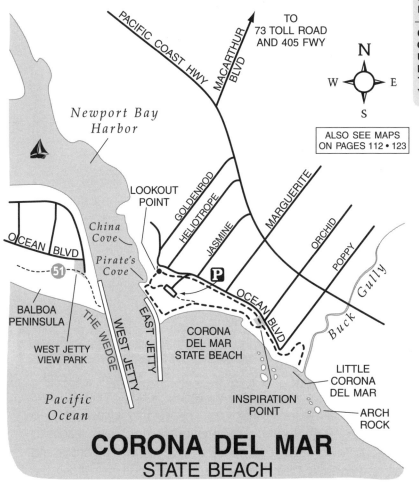

Hike 53
Back Bay Drive
UPPER NEWPORT BAY ECOLOGICAL RESERVE

Hiking distance: 4.6 miles round trip
Hiking time: 2 hours
Elevation gain: 100 feet
Maps: U.S.G.S. Newport Beach and Tustin
     Franko's Map of Newport Bay

Summary of hike: Back Bay Drive follows the east shore of the Upper Newport Bay Ecological Reserve, where the ocean's salt water mixes with nutrient-rich freshwater from San Diego Creek, the Santa Ana Delhi Channel, and various side streams. The 752-acre wetland is the largest remaining estuary in southern California. The preserve is renowned as one of the finest birding sites in North America. This hike follows a paved multiuse road for hikers, bikers, and occasional one-way vehicles. The road hugs the east edge of the wetland sanctuary along the base of 100-foot eroding sandstone cliffs.

Driving directions: From the 405 (San Diego) Freeway in Irvine, take the Jamboree Road exit. Drive 4.2 miles south to San Joaquin Hills Road and turn right. Continue 0.3 miles to Back Bay Drive. Park on San Joaquin Hills Road or in the pullouts on Back Bay Drive.

Hiking directions: Head north on the road/trail along the east edge of the wetland preserve below the sandstone cliffs. At a quarter mile, the winding path reaches an overlook of the Upper and Middle Islands to the west, across from stream-fed Big Canyon to the east. A half-mile loop on the right tours a freshwater pond and marsh in Big Canyon. Staying on Back Bay Drive, cross the canyon spillway and follow the contours of the estuary. At 1.5 miles, ascend a gentle rise to a gravel walkway and overlook with interpretive panels about the waterfowl. At just over 2 miles, climb the 100-foot cliffs to the blufftop at

Eastbluff Drive. On the left is an overlook of the estuary. Return along the same trail.

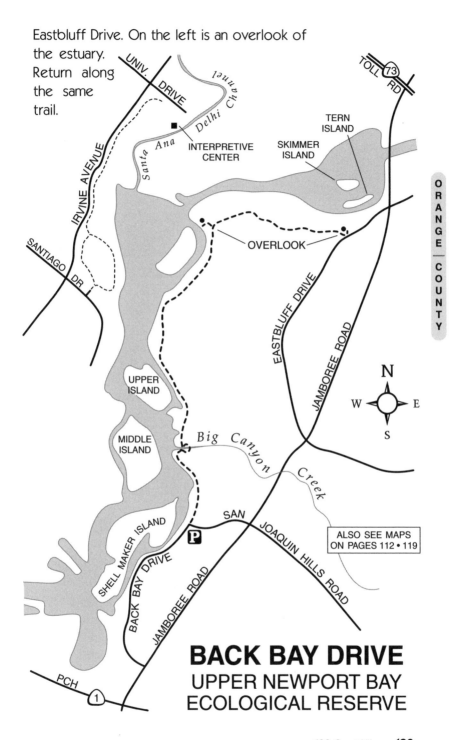

BACK BAY DRIVE
UPPER NEWPORT BAY
ECOLOGICAL RESERVE

ALSO SEE MAPS
ON PAGES 112 • 119

Hike 54
Crystal Cove Oceanfront Bluffs
CRYSTAL COVE STATE PARK

Hiking distance: 0.5 to 6 miles round trip
Hiking time: 15 minutes to 3 hours
Elevation gain: 100 feet
Maps: U.S.G.S. Laguna Beach
      Crystal Cove State Park map

Summary of hike: Crystal Cove State Park offers 3.25 miles of unobstructed, scenic coastline between Corona Del Mar and Laguna Beach. The oceanfront park is lined with an ancient 50- to 100-foot tall marine terrace, supporting coastal sage scrub and grasses. The cliff-sheltered sandy beach has rocky coves, tidepools, reefs, and is a designated underwater marine life refuge. The beach is a premier destination for swimming, surfing, snorkeling, and diving. The state park has 3 blufftop parking lots and 8 beach accesses. Trails cross the bluffs the entire length of the park and lead down to the scalloped coastline and pocket beaches. This hike can be as short or long as you choose, as you may hike a variety of bluff-to-beach loops.

Driving directions: From the 405 (San Diego) Freeway on the west end of Irvine, take the Jamboree Road exit. Drive 1.6 miles south to Macarthur Boulevard and turn left. Continue 4 miles to the Pacific Coast Highway and turn left. Drive 2.1 miles to Pelican Point Drive and turn right into the signed Crystal Cove State Park. A parking fee is required.

From the 405 (San Diego) Freeway on the east end of Irvine, take the Laguna Canyon Road (Highway 133) exit and drive 8.2 miles south to the Pacific Coast Highway. Turn right and continue 4.7 miles to Pelican Point Drive. Turn left into Crystal Cove State Park.

Hiking directions: The PELICAN POINT parking lot is the northernmost entrance of the state park. Paved and meandering natural paths parallel the crenulated coastal bluffs, with expansive views of offshore rocks, Catalina Island, Newport Beach, Long Beach, and Abalone Point. A concrete ramp leads down the sedimentary cliffs to the beach and tidepools off Pelican Point.

The LOS TRANCOS parking lot is located a half mile south of the Pelican Point entrance on the inland side of the PCH. A paved walking road leads in two directions from the southeast corner of the lot, dropping into Los Trancos Canyon. The two routes merge near the PCH at a beach access tunnel built in 1932. Cross under the highway, emerging in a grove of eucalyptus, sycamores, and palms. The right fork climbs up to the bluffs towards Pelican Point. The left fork follows Los Trancos Canyon into the Crystal Cove Historic District, a small community of charming wood-frame cottages built in the late 1920s and 1930s. Just past the cottages, at the mouth of the canyon, is the sandy beachfront beneath the 100-foot sandstone cliffs.

The REEF POINT parking lot is located 1.6 miles south of the Pelican Point entrance. From atop the bluffs, a paved path parallels the bluffs. Various natural paths meander along the cliff's edge, reconnecting with the main path. Paved ramps descend from each end of the parking lot to the seashore near tidepools and rock outcroppings.

CRYSTAL COVE
OCEANFRONT BLUFFS
CRYSTAL COVE STATE PARK

ORANGE COUNTY

57

1

SCHOOL

SPLIT ROCK

P REEF POINT

LOS TRANCOS CANYON

P LOS TRANCOS

CRYSTAL COVE STATE PARK

Pacific Ocean

PACIFIC COAST HWY

ENTRANCE STATION

P PELICAN POINT

TO NEWPORT BEACH

N E S W

ALSO SEE MAPS ON PAGES 112 • 129

Hike 55
El Moro Canyon—El Moro Ridge Loop
CRYSTAL COVE STATE PARK

Hiking distance: 9.5 miles round trip
Hiking time: 5 hours
Elevation gain: 900 feet
Maps: U.S.G.S. Laguna Beach
       Crystal Cove State Park map

map
next page

Summary of hike: Crystal Cove State Park is a 2,791-acre oceanfront park between Laguna Beach and Corona Del Mar. The state park includes 2,200 inland acres in the San Joaquin Hills, rising 1,100 feet from the coastal plain to the ridge in only 3 miles. The park encompasses the El Moro Canyon watershed and all the adjoining drainages. The undeveloped backcountry has hiking, biking, and equestrian trails that lead up wooded canyons and across 1,000-foot high ridges. This loop hike ascends El Moro Canyon through riparian woodlands with sycamores, willows, and live oaks. It returns on El Moro Ridge through chaparral, coastal sage scrub, and grasslands.

Driving directions: From the 405 (San Diego) Freeway on the west end of Irvine, take the Jamboree Road exit. Drive 1.6 miles south to Macarthur Boulevard and turn left. Continue 4 miles to the Pacific Coast Highway and turn left. Drive 4 miles to El Moro Canyon. Turn left, then curve left on the frontage road past the school. Turn right, curving a quarter mile into the Crystal Cove State Park parking lot and ranger station. A parking fee is required.

    From the 405 (San Diego) Freeway on the east end of Irvine, take the Laguna Canyon Road (Highway 133) exit, and drive 8.2 miles south to the Pacific Coast Highway. Turn right and follow the directions above.

Hiking directions: Walk downhill to the parking lot entrance, and bear left (south) on the posted fire road/trail. Skirt a trailer park, and drop into El Moro Canyon. Cross the seasonal stream to a signed junction with the B.F.I. Trail at 0.5 miles. Begin the loop to the left, heading up the canyon floor. Pass the East Cut-Across Trail on the right and the West Cut-Across Trail 100 yards ahead. Curve up the west-facing hillside to an overlook of sedimentary rock formations in a side canyon. Drop down into the canyon under oaks and sycamores to a junction with the Slow N' Easy Trail. Stay in the canyon to a Y-split. Take the steep right fork, climbing along the power poles to Bommer Ridge. Bear right and cross the head of El Moro Canyon, just beneath the ridge. At the junction, the left fork continues to Laguna Coast Wilderness Park. Bear right on El Moro Ridge, straddling Emerald and El Moro Canyons. Pass the Upper Moro Ridge Campground on a grassy flat, and continue to an old asphalt road at the Lower Moro Ridge Campground. Follow the old road to the left, passing the East Cut-Across Trail to the right. Stay on the ridge, and cross under power poles to a trail fork 200 yards ahead. Bear right on the B.F.I. Trail and wind downhill, with phenomenal coastal views of Abalone Point and Emerald Bay. Complete the loop in the canyon and return to the left.

Hike 56
Emerald Canyon—Bommer Ridge Loop
LAGUNA COAST WILDERNESS PARK
20101 Laguna Canyon Road · Laguna Beach
Open Saturday and Sunday · 7:00 a.m. to sunset

Hiking distance: 6.5 miles round trip
Hiking time: 3.5 hours
Elevation gain: 1,400 feet
Maps: U.S.G.S. Laguna Beach
Laguna Coast Wilderness Park map

map
next page

Summary of hike: Laguna Coast Wilderness Park is a diverse 6,500-acre undeveloped parkland between Laguna Canyon and Crystal Cove State Park, stretching inland from Laguna Beach to Irvine. Once a working cattle ranch, it is now a protected natural landscape, part of the 38,000-acre South Coast

Wilderness. This hike loops through coastal canyons and high open ridges in the heart of the parkland. The route follows tree-shaded Willow and Emerald Canyons, passing weather-carved rock formations and meadows. The hike also includes Emerald and Bommer Ridges, with panoramic vistas of the ocean, coastline, and San Joaquin Hills.

Driving directions: From the 405 (San Diego) Freeway in Irvine, take the Laguna Canyon Road (Highway 133) exit, and drive 5 miles south to the signed Laguna Coast Wilderness parking lot on the right, just south of the El Toro Road intersection.

From the Pacific Coast Highway in downtown Laguna Beach, head 3.2 miles north on Broadway (which becomes Laguna Canyon Road) to the posted Laguna Coast Wilderness parking lot on the left.

Hiking directions: Start at the junction at the northwest corner of the parking lot. The footpath to the right leads to Laurel Canyon. Bear left, passing the visitor center, and head up Willow Canyon, leaving the coveted shade of sycamores and oaks. Climb the south canyon wall on a steep grade, passing large sandstone boulders. The path levels out and traverses the hillside to a junction in a saddle on Willow Ridge. The right fork descends into Laurel Canyon. Continue straight to a T-junction. Begin the loop to the right, and head 150 yards to a posted junction. Bear left on Emerald Canyon Road. Follow the ridge straddling the two forks of Emerald Canyon. Continue south over dips and rises on the gentle downhill grade, slowly descending to the canyon floor. The main trail follows the canyon through a grassy oak woodland. At an oak tree by sign-post 14, leave the road/trail and veer left on the Old Emerald Trail, a narrow footpath. Cross a footbridge and ascend the canyon wall. Curve left on a horseshoe bend, and climb to a T-junction on Bommer Ridge. Head north on the narrow ridge, passing Big Bend Trail on the right. Curve left across the head of Emerald Canyon, completing the loop at Willow Canyon Road. Go to the right and return down Willow Canyon.

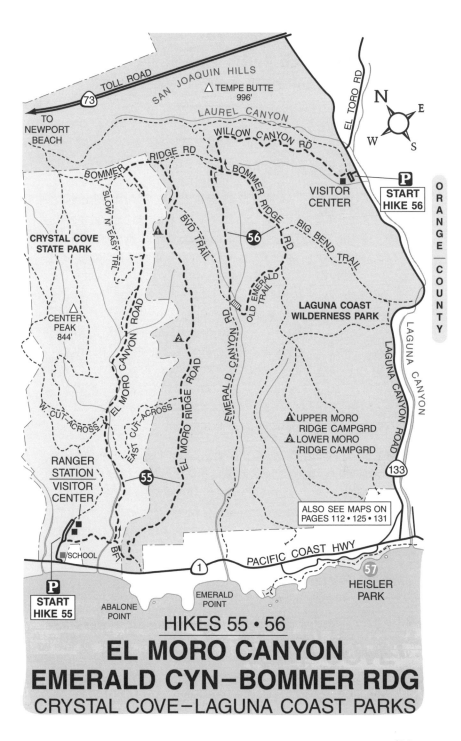

TOLL ROAD
SAN JOAQUIN HILLS
△ TEMPE BUTTE 996'
73
TO NEWPORT BEACH
LAUREL CANYON
WILLOW CANYON RD
N
E
W
S

BOMMER RIDGE RD
BOMMER RIDGE RD
VISITOR CENTER
P
START HIKE 56

CRYSTAL COVE STATE PARK
SLOW N' EASY TRL
56
BIG BEND TRAIL

BVD TRAIL
OLD EMERALD TRAIL
LAGUNA COAST WILDERNESS PARK

ORANGE COUNTY

△ CENTER PEAK 844'

EL MORO CANYON ROAD
EMERALD CANYON RD.

EL MORO RIDGE ROAD

LAGUNA CANYON ROAD
LAGUNA CANYON

W. CUT-ACROSS
EAST CUT-ACROSS

△ UPPER MORO RIDGE CAMPGRD
△ LOWER MORO RIDGE CAMPGRD

RANGER STATION VISITOR CENTER
55
133

ALSO SEE MAPS ON PAGES 112 • 125 • 131

BFT
SCHOOL

PACIFIC COAST HWY

P
START HIKE 55
ABALONE POINT
1
EMERALD POINT
57
HEISLER PARK

HIKES 55 • 56
EL MORO CANYON
EMERALD CYN–BOMMER RDG
CRYSTAL COVE–LAGUNA COAST PARKS

Hike 57
Laguna Beach Bluffs and Heisler Park
CRESCENT BAY POINT PARK TO MAIN BEACH

Hiking distance: 1.8 miles round trip
Hiking time: 1 hour
Elevation gain: 80 feet
Maps: U.S.G.S. Laguna Beach

Summary of hike: Heisler Park is a beautifully landscaped park on the cliffs above the ocean in the heart of Laguna Beach. The park sits at the base of the San Joaquin Hills, 80 feet above the scalloped coastline. The Laguna Beach Marine Life Refuge, a protected marine park with tidepools, stretches along the coast beneath Heisler Park. It is a popular area for snorkeling and diving. This hike begins in Crescent Bay Point Park, with views of Seal Rock, the rocky coastline, Catalina Island, and San Clemente Island. A paved path overlooking the magnificent seascape follows the palisades, passing a series of craggy points, sheltered sandy coves, and tidepool pockets. Paths and stairways descend to the protected coves, surrounded by steep cliffs, rock formations, and tidepools.

Driving directions: From the 405 (San Diego) Freeway in Irvine, take the Laguna Canyon Road (Highway 133) exit, and drive 8.2 miles south to the Pacific Coast Highway in downtown Laguna Beach. Turn right and drive 0.7 miles to the second Cliff Drive intersection. Turn left and park along the bluffs (metered parking).

Hiking directions: Walk to the right to Crescent Bay Point Park on the northwest end of the bay, with great views of the bay and offshore rocks. Return southeast along the bluffs, passing Twin Points, Shaw's Cove, Fisherman's Cove, and Diver's Cove. (Stairs descend to the sandy beaches in Crescent Bay and Fisherman's Cove.) Enter Heisler Park and follow the crenulated coastline under pines and palms. Continue past Picnic Beach, Recreation Point, and Rockpile Beach. Stairways lead down the eroded cliffs to the offshore rocks at the point and beach. At the west end of Cliff Drive is a cliff-edge gazebo overlooking the ocean and Bird Rock. A path on the right winds through dense foliage and rejoins the main path. Descend from the east end of the bluffs on a sloping grade and down steps to Main Beach, a sandy beach at the south end of Broadway. A wooden boardwalk snakes along the coastline between the beachfront sand and the grassy park in downtown Laguna Beach, ending at Forest Avenue. Return by retracing your steps.

ALSO SEE MAPS
ON PAGES 112 • 129

TO
SAN DIEGO FWY
AND I-5

LAGUNA CANYON RD

FOREST AVE

BROADWAY

CLIFF DR

Laguna
Beach

MAIN BEACH

BIRD ROCK

GAZEBO

HEISLER PARK

ROCKPILE BEACH

RECREATION PT

PICNIC BEACH

Diver's Cove

Fisherman's
Cove

Shaw's Cove

CLIFF DR

TWIN POINTS

P

Crescent
Bay

TWO ROCK POINT

SEAL ROCK

CRESCENT BAY
POINT PARK

LAGUNA COAST WILDERNESS PARK

PACIFIC COAST HWY

Emerald Bay

EMERALD POINT

TO
NEWPORT
BEACH

1

Pacific Ocean

O R A N G E   C O U N T Y

E

N - S

W

LAGUNA BEACH
BLUFFS
HEISLER PARK

Hike 58
West Ridge—Rock-It—Mathis Canyon Loop
ALISO AND WOOD CANYONS WILDERNESS PARK

Hiking distance: 8 miles round trip
Hiking time: 4 hours
Elevation gain: 850 feet
Maps: U.S.G.S. Laguna Beach and San Juan Capistrano
       Aliso and Wood Canyons Wilderness Park map

map
next page

Summary of hike: From Laguna Beach, the San Joaquin Hills rise abruptly from the sea to an elevation over 1,000 feet. Large undeveloped areas have been preserved as public parks and wilderness land, with an extensive network of hiking, mountain biking, and equestrian trails. One of these treasures, Aliso and Wood Canyons Wilderness Park, spreads across 4,000 acres and includes more than 30 miles of trails. The park has massive sandstone formations, several forested canyons, two year-round streams, lush riparian vegetation, oaks, elder-berries, sycamores, and native grasslands. This hike begins from the Top of the World trailhead on Temple Hill, the highest point in the park at 1,036 feet. The awesome bird's-eye views extend across the Pacific Ocean and into Laguna and Wood Canyons. The undulating path follows a ridge separating the canyons and drops into the upper end of Wood Canyon, shaded by ancient oaks and sycamores.

Driving directions: From the 405 (San Diego) Freeway in Irvine, take the Laguna Canyon Road (Highway 133) exit, and drive 8.2 miles south to the Pacific Coast Highway in downtown Laguna Beach. Turn left a few blocks to Legion Street. Turn left and drive 2 blocks to Park Avenue. Veer right onto Park Avenue, and wind 1.7 miles up the hill to Alta Laguna Boulevard at the end of the road. Turn left and continue 0.2 miles to Alta Laguna Park. Turn right and park in the lot.

Hiking directions: From the northwest corner of the park-ing lot, walk up the steps to a trail information board and a junction. Take the West Ridge Trail to the right and descend along the spine between Laguna and Wood Canyons. Cross the saddle on the narrow ridge to a posted junction with the Mathis Canyon Trail at 0.6 miles—the return route. Begin the loop to the left, staying on the ridge to a large water tank on the left and a junction on the right at 1.5 miles. Bear right on the Rock-It Trail and descend a minor ridge. The trail descends on an easy grade, then becomes steep through a slab rock section of trail. Make a sweeping left bend, and drop down into the canyon at the Coyote Run Trail at 3 miles. Curve right through an oak grove to the Wood Canyon floor. Follow the west edge of the creek to a streamside junction with the signed Mathis Canyon Trail. Bear right, leaving the creek, and head uphill. Curve around the west flank of the hillside by sandstone caves. Pass the Oak Grove Trail on the left, and climb up a steep grade to an overlook of Oak Grove. Walk through a trail gate and steeply climb up the ridge, completing the loop on the ridge. Bear left and return to Alta Laguna Park.

Hike 59
Aliso Canyon and Wood Canyon
ALISO AND WOOD CANYONS WILDERNESS PARK
28373 Alicia Parkway · Laguna Niguel

Hiking distance: 5.7 miles round trip
Hiking time: 3 hours
Elevation gain: 150 feet
Maps: U.S.G.S. San Juan Capistrano
Aliso and Wood Canyons Wilderness Park map

map next page

Summary of hike: Aliso and Wood Canyons Wilderness Park is pristine parkland tucked into the hillsides and valleys between Laguna Beach, Laguna Niguel, and Aliso Viejo. The undeveloped refuge has two major stream-fed canyons, sandstone formations, caves sculpted by wind and water, aged groves of live oaks and sycamores, and an extensive hiking and biking trail system. This hike travels west into Aliso Canyon and turns north up Wood Canyon. Along the way, the trail passes Cave Rock, a 26-million-year-old sandstone formation, and Dripping Cave, a historic water-carved cave also known as Robber's Cave. The overhanging rock shelter was used as a hideout to rob stagecoaches en route from San Diego to Los Angeles. Holes are bored into the interior sandstone walls, once used for hanging supplies on pegs.

Driving directions: From the I-5 (San Diego) Freeway in Laguna Hills, take the Alicia Parkway exit, and head 4 miles south to the posted Aliso and Wood Canyons Wilderness Park on the right. (The turnoff is a quarter mile south of Aliso Creek Road.) Turn right and park in the lot on the left. A parking fee is required.

Hiking directions: Walk past the museum to the gated park road. Descend into open Aliso Canyon, filled with grasses, sage, and chaparral. Follow the footpath that parallels the right side of the road to the end of the access road at 1.5 miles, where Aliso and Wood Canyons join. Bear right and pass through a trail gate into Wood Canyon. Head up the canyon, reaching the posted Cave Rock Trail. Bear left on the quarter-mile loop, and cross the grassy meadow to the south edge of the enormous rock. Detour along the west edge of the formation by numerous caves. Return to the south edge and follow the trail up the rock's low spine to the summit. Slowly descend and curve around the north end of the rock, rejoining the Wood Canyon Trail. Continue up canyon on the west side of Wood Creek to the Dripping Cave junction. Bear left and detour 350 yards into a shady oak grove and the water-carved cave. Returning to the main trail, cross a stream spillway to a signed junction at the mouth of Mathis Canyon. A short distance ahead is an old sheep corral, originally used by the Moulton Ranch family. This is our turnaround spot.

To hike further, the path meanders up the canyon, connecting with the Lynx and Cholla Trails leading up to the West Ridge Trail (Hike 58).

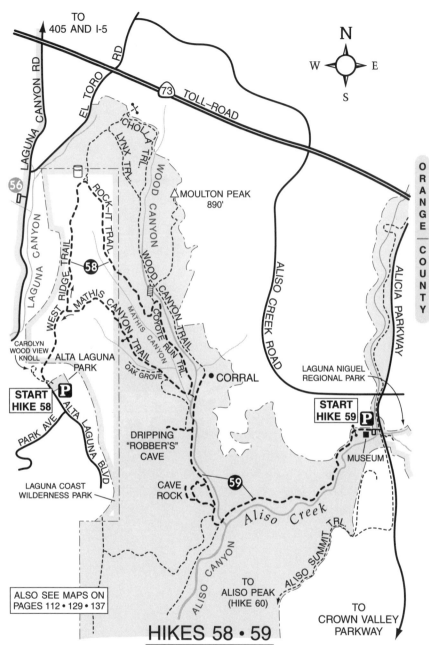

TO
405 AND I-5

N
W E
S

LAGUNA CANYON RD

EL TORO RD

73 TOLL-ROAD

ORANGE COUNTY

CHOLLA TRL.

LYNX TRL.

WOOD CANYON

△ MOULTON PEAK
890'

ALISO CREEK ROAD

ALICIA PARKWAY

56

ROCK-IT TRAIL

LAGUNA CANYON

58

WEST RIDGE TRAIL

WOOD CANYON TRAIL

MATHIS CANYON TRAIL

MATHIS CANYON

COYOTE RUN TRL.

CAROLYN
WOOD VIEW
KNOLL

ALTA LAGUNA
PARK

OAK GROVE

• CORRAL

LAGUNA NIGUEL
REGIONAL PARK

START
HIKE 58
P

ALTA LAGUNA BLVD

PARK AVE

START
HIKE 59
P

DRIPPING
"ROBBER'S"
CAVE

MUSEUM

LAGUNA COAST
WILDERNESS PARK

CAVE
ROCK

59

Aliso Creek

ALSO SEE MAPS ON
PAGES 112 • 129 • 137

ALISO CANYON

ALISO SUMMIT TRL.

TO
ALISO PEAK
(HIKE 60)

TO
CROWN VALLEY
PARKWAY

HIKES 58 • 59

ALISO AND WOOD CANYONS
WILDERNESS PARK

Hike 60
Aliso Peak Trail from Seaview Park

Hiking distance: 0.5—2.8 miles round trip
Hiking time: 30 minutes—1.5 hours
Elevation gain: Level to 400 feet
Maps: U.S.G.S. San Juan Capistrano
　　　　Aliso and Wood Canyons Wilderness Park map

Summary of hike: Seaview Park straddles the crest of Niguel Hill on the east boundary of Aliso and Wood Canyons Wilderness Park. The ridge-top park sits on the cliffs 800 feet above Aliso Canyon and borders a residential neighborhood. At the west end of the park is the Seaview Park Overlook, a platform with interpretive displays perched on the ridge. The sweeping vistas overlook the South Coast Wilderness Parks in the San Joaquin Hills, Aliso Canyon, Laguna Beach, the scalloped coastline, the communities across Saddleback Valley, and the Santa Ana Mountains. The trail follows the oceanfront ridge to Aliso Peak, where the hill dramatically drops 623 feet into the sea.

Driving directions: From I-5 (San Diego Freeway) in Laguna Niguel, take the Crown Valley Parkway exit, and head 5.3 miles south to Pacific Island Drive. Turn right and drive 1.6 miles to the crest of the hill, then turn left on Talavera Drive. Continue a quarter mile and park along the curb near the end of the road.

From the Pacific Coast Highway, drive 0.8 miles north on Crown Valley Parkway to Pacific Island Drive on the left.

Hiking directions: Walk west along Seaview Park's grassy strip, hugging the edge of the 800-foot cliffs on the south rim of Aliso Canyon. The views extend up and down the canyon and across the valley basin to the Santa Ana Mountains. Leave the grassy parkland into the native chaparral and coastal sage scrub, topping a small rise to a view of Catalina Island. Curve west and follow the ridge past the interpretive panels to a picnic table at the Seaview Park Overlook. This is a good turnaround spot for a short, half-mile hike. Aliso Peak Trail, a narrow footpath, continues downhill, dropping to a saddle by a road in a gated community. Veer away from the road, and drop down to a lower saddle. Cross the saddle, staying on the ridge to a trail split. Stay to the right, rising slightly to Aliso Peak. From the peak are sweeping 360-degree coastal views as far as the haze allows.

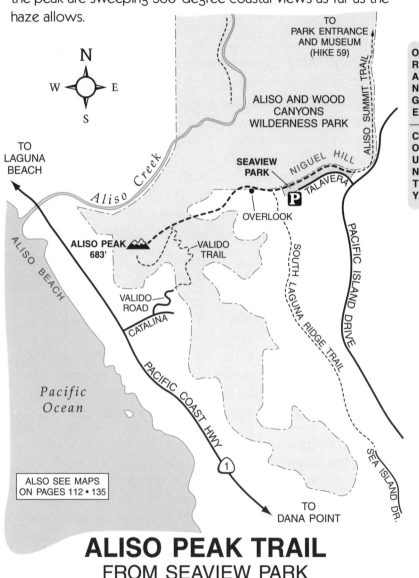

ALISO PEAK TRAIL
FROM SEAVIEW PARK

Hike 61
Salt Creek Beach Park

Hiking distance: 2 miles round trip
Hiking time: 1 hour
Elevation gain: 80 feet
Maps: U.S.G.S. Dana Point

Summary of hike: Salt Creek Beach Park is a 1.5-mile-long beach strand that stretches between Dana Point and Three Arch Cove in South Laguna. The popular surfing beach is divided by a point, on which the Ritz Carlton Hotel is perched. A paved pedestrian path leads through the Ritz Carlton Hotel grounds to Bluff Park, a 7-acre sloping grassland park with benches and picnic tables that overlook the beach. It is a great spot to view migrating gray whales and Catalina Island. A paved path follows the bluffs, with stairways and paths leading down to the beach. At the north end, the path connects with the Salt Creek Trail (Hike 62), a multi-use trail heading inland along Salt Creek.

Driving directions: From I-5 (San Diego Freeway) in San Juan Capistrano, take the Beach Cities/Highway 1 exit, and head 3.7 miles west to Ritz Carlton Drive. Turn left and drive 0.1 miles to the Salt Creek Beach parking lot on the left. A parking fee is required.

From I-5 (San Diego Freeway) in Laguna Niguel, take the Crown Valley Parkway exit, and head 6.1 miles south to the Pacific Coast Highway. Turn left and continue 0.7 miles to Ritz Carlton Drive. Turn right and drive 0.1 miles to the Salt Creek Beach parking lot on the left.

Hiking directions: From the south end of the parking lot, take the park road under Ritz Carlton Drive to the expansive, sloping parkland overlooking the ocean. As you near the bluffs, a paved path heads south (left) and climbs the bluffs through the landscaped hotel grounds to an overlook. The views extend from the Dana Point promontory to Catalina Island to the San Joaquin Hills backing South Laguna. Return to the park road at the beachfront. Head north on the paved blufftop path. Continue through Bluff Park towards the headland at Three Arch Cove. Just before reaching the golf course, a couple of unpaved sloping paths lead down to the beach. To hike further, the Salt Creek Trail (Hike 62) continues inland along the edge of the golf course and through a tunnel under the Pacific Coast Highway. To return, curve left, leaving the bluff path to the lower path at the back edge of the sandy beach. Return on the oceanfront path to the beach access trail. The path continues south, ending at the sand.

O R A N G E | C O U N T Y

TO
SOUTH
LAGUNA

TO
SALT CREEK
REGIONAL
PARK

1

62

Salt Cr.

THREE
ARCH
COVE

MONARCH BEACH

THE LINKS
AT MONARCH
BEACH

N

W ⊕ E

S

BLUFF
PARK

SALT CREEK

PACIFIC COAST HWY

RITZ CARLTON

P

NIGUEL
ROAD

DR

Pacific
Ocean

SALT CREEK BEACH PARK

RITZ
CARLTON

OVERLOOK

ALSO SEE MAPS
ON PAGES 112 • 141

SALT CREEK
BEACH PARK

100 Great Hikes - **139**

Hike 62
Salt Creek Trail

Hiking distance: 6 miles round trip
Hiking time: 3 hours
Elevation gain: 400 feet
Maps: U.S.G.S. Dana Point and San Juan Capistrano

Summary of hike: The Salt Creek watershed flows through the cities of Laguna Niguel and Dana Point to the sea. A paved three-mile, multi-use trail follows Salt Creek through a wide greenbelt corridor in the heart of Laguna Niguel, connecting the beach with the coastal hills. This hike begins from Salt Creek Beach Park (Hike 61) between South Laguna and Dana Point at the Ritz Carlton Hotel grounds. From the north end of beach, the paved path curves inland, heading through The Links at Monarch Beach, Salt Creek Regional Park, and San Juan Canyon to Chapparosa Community Park.

Driving directions: Same as Hike 61.

Hiking directions: Follow the Salt Creek Beach (Hike 61) hiking directions to the north end of the oceanfront bluff path. (See map on page 139.) Curve inland along the north edge of the golf course and through a tunnel under the Pacific Coast Highway. Head up the wide canyon on a steady but gentle uphill grade along the north side of Salt Creek. As you near Camino Del Avion, curve right and pass under the road to a trail split. The right fork leads up to the road. Stay left, parallel Camino Del Avion a short distance, and curve right on the rim of the canyon above Salt Creek. The undulating path winds through the natural open canyon for the next mile. As you near Niguel Road at the Clubhouse Plaza Shops, make an S-curve, passing through the Niguel Road tunnel. Continue on the north slope of San Juan Canyon to the grassy picnic area with sycamore groves, rolling hills, and baseball fields at Chapparosa Community Park. Return by retracing your steps.

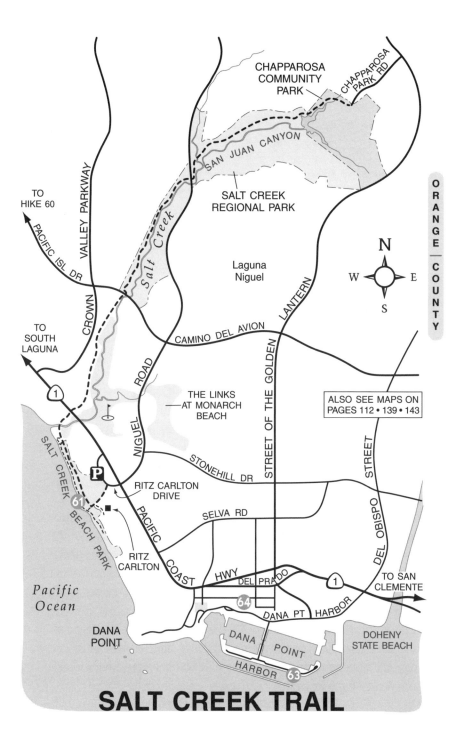

CHAPPAROSA COMMUNITY PARK

CHAPPAROSA PARK RD

TO HIKE 60

PACIFIC ISL DR

VALLEY PARKWAY

San Juan Canyon

SALT CREEK REGIONAL PARK

Salt Creek

Laguna Niguel

LANTERN

ORANGE COUNTY

N
W   E
S

TO SOUTH LAGUNA

CROWN

CAMINO DEL AVION

STREET OF THE GOLDEN

NIGUEL ROAD

THE LINKS AT MONARCH BEACH

ALSO SEE MAPS ON PAGES 112 • 139 • 143

STONEHILL DR

P

61

RITZ CARLTON DRIVE

SELVA RD

PACIFIC COAST HWY

DEL OBISPO STREET

SALT CREEK BEACH PARK

RITZ CARLTON

DEL PRADO

1

TO SAN CLEMENTE

Pacific Ocean

64

DANA PT HARBOR

DANA POINT

DANA POINT

DOHENY STATE BEACH

HARBOR

63

SALT CREEK TRAIL

Hike 63
Dana Point Harbor

Hiking distance: 2.5 miles round trip
Hiking time: 1.5 hours
Elevation gain: Level
Maps: U.S.G.S. Dana Point

Summary of hike: Dana Point Harbor, built in 1971, is a majestic harbor located at the base of 200-foot cliffs. The harbor lies between the 120-acre Dana Point headland and Doheny State Beach. The Dana Point Marine Life Refuge surrounds the steep precipice from the west end of the harbor, including the offshore San Juan Rocks. Tidepools line the protected refuge, with sea urchins, anemones, starfish, and hermit crabs. A grassy waterfront park with picnic tables, a calm-water swimming beach, fishing platforms, and a paved walkway border the marina. Dana Island, a picturesque manmade island park, is reached via Island Way, a vehicle-pedestrian bridge beside the boat moorings. This hike explores the harbor from beneath the Dana Point cliffs to Dana Island.

Driving directions: From I-5 (San Diego Freeway) in San Juan Capistrano, take the Beach Cities/Highway 1 exit, and head 1.3 miles west to Dana Point Harbor Drive. Turn left and continue 1.1 miles to the posted pier parking lot on the left.

Hiking directions: From the grassy beachfront park, take the paved path to the right, looping around the west end of the marina. Pass a few wooden piers, the ocean institute, and a bookstore to the mile-long breakwater. At the far west end of the harbor, just past the rock jetty, steps lead down to a fenced enclosure. Pass through the open structure to the shoreline at the base of the 200-foot cliffs. Follow the base of the cliffs just above the rocky beach towards Dana Point. At low tide, the promontory can be circled, but use extreme caution. After exploring the tidepools, return to the grassy park and beach cove by the parking lot and continue east. Pass the boat moorings 0.3 miles to Island Way. Head south on the walk-way, towards the sea, and cross the 150-foot long bridge over the water channel to Dana Island. A loop path circles the narrow island that fronts the harbor channel and oceanfront.

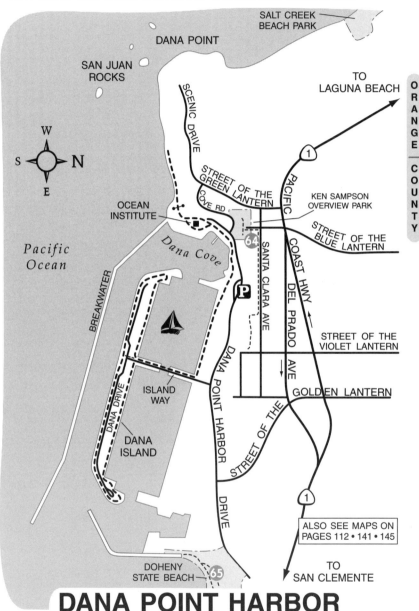

DANA POINT HARBOR

Hike 64
Hide "Blufftop" Trail
DANA POINT BLUFFS

Hiking distance: 1 mile round trip
Hiking time: 40 minutes
Elevation gain: 25 feet
Maps: U.S.G.S. Dana Point

Summary of hike: The town of Dana Point is a small, bustling enclave with a unique history. In 1835, Richard Henry Dana, aboard the brig *Pilgrim*, helped deliver goods from Boston around Cape Horn in exchange for cattle hides from Mission San Juan Capistrano. In 1840, he published his experiences in *Two Years Before the Mast*. His classic memoirs describe how the hides were thrown off the 200-foot cliffs from the current site of the Ken Sampson Overview to the beach below, where longboats rowed them out to the ship. The Hide Trail clings to the 200-foot cliffs from Ken Sampson Overview Park. The interpretive trail has informational plaques about Richard Henry Dana and a larger-than-life statue of a hide drogher, tossing hides off the cliffs. The trail passes an arched concrete wall and winding stone-lined paths, remnants of an abandoned hotel from the early 1930s. The coastal views extend across Capistrano Bay from Dana Point to San Mateo Point.

Driving directions: From I-5 (San Diego Freeway) in San Juan Capistrano, take the Beach Cities/Highway 1 exit, and head 2.4 miles west to Street of the Ruby Lantern. Turn left and drive to the end of the street at Santa Clara Avenue. Turn either way and park alongside the street.

Hiking directions: Walk west on Santa Clara to the corner at Street of the Blue Lantern. Bear left to Ken Sampson Overview Park and the gazebo extending off the cliffs, over- looking the Dana Point headland; the harbor; Doheny, Capistrano, and San Clemente Beaches; and San Mateo Point at the southern county line. Walk inland to Santa Clara Avenue, the first street, and go one block east (right) to Street of the Amber Lantern. Return to the edge of the cliffs at another overlook. Take the posted Hide Trail east, which follows an early native Indian route. Traverse the cliffs and cross a deep gorge on a wooden footbridge to a cement archway. Notice the remnants of a rock path that once led to the Dana Point Inn, dating back to the early 1930s. Cross under the archway and climb steps to a sandstone rock wall and a 9-foot bronze statue of a hide droghing seaman. The trail ends at an overlook at the corner of Street of the Violet Lantern and El Camino Capistrano. Return by retracing your steps.

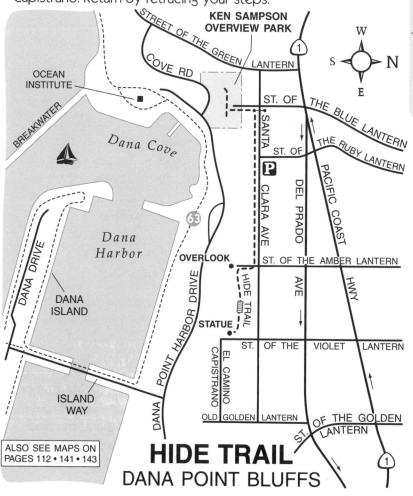

HIDE TRAIL
DANA POINT BLUFFS

ALSO SEE MAPS ON PAGES 112 • 141 • 143

Hike 65
Doheny State Beach • Capistrano Beach Park
25300 Dana Point Harbor Drive • Dana Point

Hiking distance: 2.8 miles round trip
Hiking time: 1.5 hours
Elevation gain: Level
Maps: U.S.G.S. Dana Point

Summary of hike: Doheny State Beach and Capistrano Beach Park merge into an unbroken 3-mile strand of white sand beach between Dana Point Harbor and San Clemente. Doheny State Beach is a 62-acre beach park at the mouth of San Juan Creek, with over a mile of sandy beachfront. During the summer, a sandbar restrains the creek's flow into the sea, forming a lagoon and bird sanctuary. West of the creek is a 5-acre landscaped picnic area with shady trees, a rocky area with tidepools, and a visitor center with simulated tidepools and aquariums. The Doheny Marine Life Refuge, popular with divers, is an offshore underwater park. East of San Juan Creek is a wooded campground with 121 developed campsites. To the north, a bike path heads inland to San Juan Capistrano on a levee parallel to the west side of the creek. A palm-lined walkway connects Doheny State Beach with Capistrano Beach Park, backed by a 120-foot marine terrace. Two pedestrian overpasses cross over the highway from the beach to the palisades.

Driving directions: From I-5 (San Diego Freeway) in San Juan Capistrano, take the Beach Cities/Highway 1 exit, and head 1.3 miles west to Dana Point Harbor Drive. Turn left and continue 0.1 miles to the posted Doheny State Beach entrance on the left. Turn left and park in the enormous parking lot, just past the park entrance and visitor center. An entrance fee is required.

Hiking directions: Head west, strolling through the lush grassland park dotted with eucalyptus and palm trees. Continue to the tidepools at the state beach boundary by the rock jetty enclosing Dana Point Harbor (Hike 63). Return to the east on the paved path, following the coastline between the grassy picnic area and the wide, crescent-shaped sandy beach. At San Juan Creek, cross the sandbar at the mouth of the river. If the sandbar has been breached, curve inland on the paved path and parallel the creek to the park road. Cross the creek on the bridge, and return to the beachfront. Stroll along the palm-lined beach, with views of Dana Point, the harbor, and the oceanfront cliffs. At one mile, a pedestrian bridge crosses over the Pacific Coast Highway, connecting to the inland shops. Doheny State Beach ends a quarter mile beyond the bridge. A walkway near the highway leads into Capistrano Beach Park. At 1.4 miles, a short distance ahead, a row of houses line the top of the beach. This is our turn-around spot.

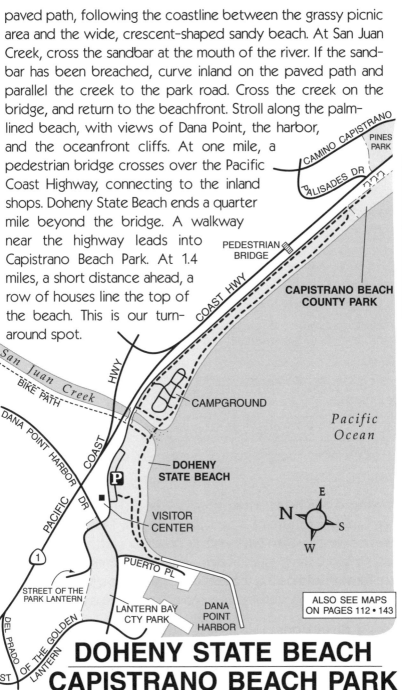

ALSO SEE MAPS ON PAGES 112 • 143

DOHENY STATE BEACH
CAPISTRANO BEACH PARK

Hike 66
San Clemente State Beach to San Mateo Point

Hiking distance: 3 miles round trip
Hiking time: 1.5 hours
Elevation gain: 100 feet
Maps: U.S.G.S. San Clemente

map
next page

Summary of hike: San Clemente State Beach is the southern-most beach in Orange County. The secluded 1.5-mile coastal stretch sits beneath craggy 100-foot sandstone cliffs with eroded gullies and railroad tracks chiseled along the base of the bluffs. Atop the coastal terrace is the developed state beach campground and picnic area, landscaped with palms, acacias, cypress, sycamores, and other exotics. Two trails descend the 100-foot bluffs through eroded ravines, from the campground to the isolated, sandy beach. To the north is Calafia Beach Park, a day-use area at the foot of Avenida Calafia. The beach provides a pedestrian crossing over the railroad tracks. This loop hike follows the coastline from Calafia Beach Park to San Mateo Point and returns along the top of the bluffs. The beach strand passes former President Nixon's Western White House. It was also used during his retreat into isolation after resigning from office. The Spanish-style stucco home with a red tile roof sits on 25 blufftop acres, obscured but recognizable by a dense cover of palm trees.

Driving directions: Heading southbound on I-5 (San Diego Freeway) in San Clemente, take the Avenida Calafia exit. Drive 0.4 miles west to the Calafia Beach oceanfront parking lot. The parking is metered.

Heading northbound on I-5 (San Diego Freeway) in San Clemente, take the Cristianitos Road exit. Turn left and cross over the freeway to Avenida Del Presidente. Turn right and drive 1 mile to Avenida Calafia. Turn left and continue 0.4 miles to the Calafia Beach oceanfront parking lot.

Hiking directions: Two parallel routes head south along the oceanfront. Either take the undulating footpath above the railroad tracks, at the base of the eroding cliffs; or cross the railroad tracks, down an embankment, and stroll along the sandy beach beneath the rock wall. Pass a trail crossing through a tunnel under the railroad tracks. (The paths wind up the eroding gorges to the state beach campground atop the bluffs.) Continue south, following a low ridge for a quarter mile, to where the two routes merge. Stroll past oceanfront homes sitting on top of the cliffs. The distinctive, tropical landscape of former President Richard Nixon's home sets it apart. As you round San Mateo Point, the cliffs begin to level out at Trestles Beach (Hike 67). Curve inland, crossing the low dunes and railroad tracks. Head up the paved beach access through oaks and sycamores to the Old Coast Highway, a biking route closed to vehicles. Bear left up the road to Avenida Del Presidente, the west frontage road of I-5. Walk 0.8 miles north to the forested campground on the left by Avenida San Luis Rey. Take the pedestrian path through the campground, and either follow the park road to Calafia Avenue or wind down the bluffs on the beach access trail. Return to the right.

Hike 67
Trestles Beach
SAN ONOFRE STATE BEACH NORTH

Hiking distance: 2 miles round trip
Hiking time: 1 hour
Elevation gain: 100 feet
Maps: U.S.G.S. San Clemente

map
next page

Summary of hike: Trestles Beach straddles the Orange-San Diego County line at Mateo Point, on the north end of San Onofre State Beach. San Mateo Creek empties into the sea just south of the point after draining from the Santa Ana Mountains through Riverside, Orange, and San Diego Counties. The intermittent creek is a vital riparian corridor and natural preserve, forming a lagoon at the mouth of the creek. The wide, slanted beach is named for the old train trestle crossing over San Mateo Creek. It is a well-known and popular surfing spot. An unpaved trail begins on the south edge of San Clemente and leads about a mile to the beach. The trail crosses the Old Coast Highway (now a biking path beginning at Avenida Del Presidente) and continues through the San Onofre Bluffs Campground and Camp Pendleton to Oceanside. The beach resides in the shadow of San Onofre Nuclear Power Plant just two miles south. The two ominous reactor spheres loom over the coastal landscape.

Driving directions: From I-5 (San Diego Freeway) in San Clemente, take the Cristianitos Road exit. Head east one block to El Camino Real. Turn left and park along the street or in the parking area on the right.

Hiking directions: Walk back to Cristianitos Road. Take the "beach access" trail across the street on the left side of the chain-link fence. Follow the wide dirt path south, overlooking the agricultural fields and the Pacific Ocean. Descend into the forested drainage and cross under I-5. Emerge on the Old Coast Highway (now closed to vehicles) by the sign for San Onofre State Beach, Trestles Beach, and San Mateo Creek Nature Preserve. Cross the abandoned road. Take the paved beach access road, winding through native grass, chaparral, oaks, and sycamores. Cross over the railroad tracks or under the trestle to the low dunes and sandy beachfront, just north of San Mateo Point. To the north are views of San Clemente, the state beach, and the pier. To the south are views of the Santa Margarita Mountains, Camp Pendleton, and the San Onofre Bluffs. Strolling a short distance north is a view of former President Nixon's Western White House, where he retreated after his resignation (Hike 66). Return by retracing your steps.

For a longer hike, continue with Hike 66 along San Clemente State Beach.

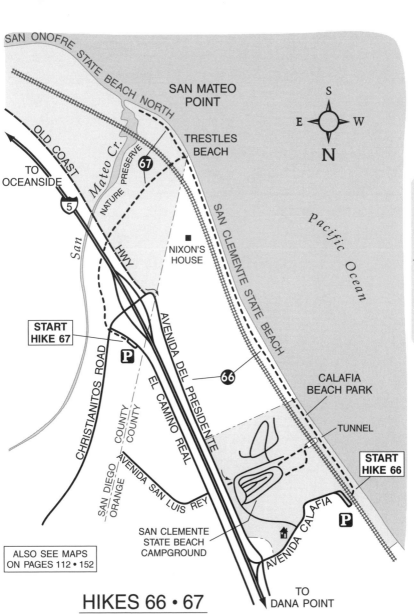

HIKES 66 • 67

SAN CLEMENTE STATE BEACH

TO SAN MATEO POINT

TRESTLES BEACH

SAN ONOFRE STATE BEACH NORTH

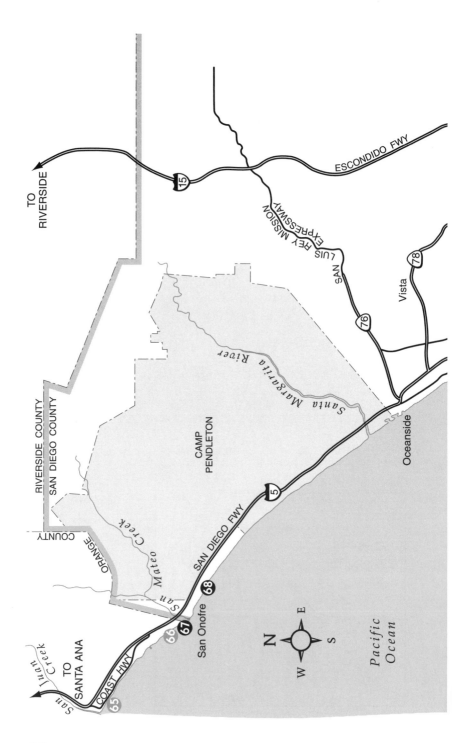

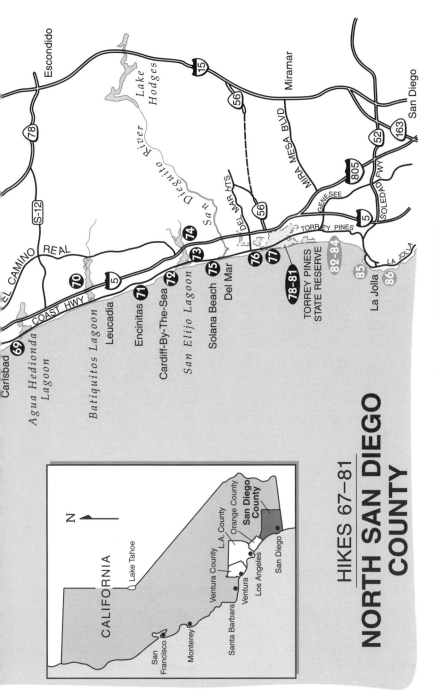

HIKES 67–81
NORTH SAN DIEGO COUNTY

Hike 68
San Onofre Bluffs
SAN ONOFRE STATE BEACH SOUTH

Hiking distance: 6 mile loop
Hiking time: 3 hours
Elevation gain: 140 feet
Maps: U.S.G.S. San Onofre Bluff

Summary of hike: The San Onofre Bluffs stretch along three miles of coastline on the south end of San Onofre State Beach, surrounded by the Camp Pendleton Marine Base. A campground sits along the picturesque coastal terrace with sweeping views. The campground road is the Old Coast Highway (Highway 101), which runs along the sheer sandstone bluffs. (The old road is also a bike path from San Clemente through Camp Pendleton to Oceanside.) Six numbered access trails cross and descend the eroding cliffs to a primitive beach with sandy coves and pockets. Between the trail accesses is a 2.6-mile strand of untamed, remote, pristine beach. The long, sandy strand is shielded from civilization by dramatic 140-foot cliffs. On the south end, at the base of Trail 6, is an unofficial clothing-optional beach. To the north lie the ever-present, surreal twin-dome reactors of the San Onofre Nuclear Power Plant.

Driving directions: From I-5 (San Diego Freeway) in San Onofre, take the Basilone Road exit. Turn southwest to the ocean side of the freeway, and drive 2.9 miles south on Old Highway 101 (the frontage road) to the San Onofre State Beach Bluffs Campground entrance. An entrance fee is required.

Hiking directions: A trail parallels the entire 3-mile length of the campground and bluffs. The six numbered trails connect to the bluff path and parking lot. Each access path heads west across the bluffs and descends to the sandy beach. Every trail is different with its own distinct character. Most have a bench at the edge of the cliffs. Trail 5 descends through a gorge. Choose your own route and distance.

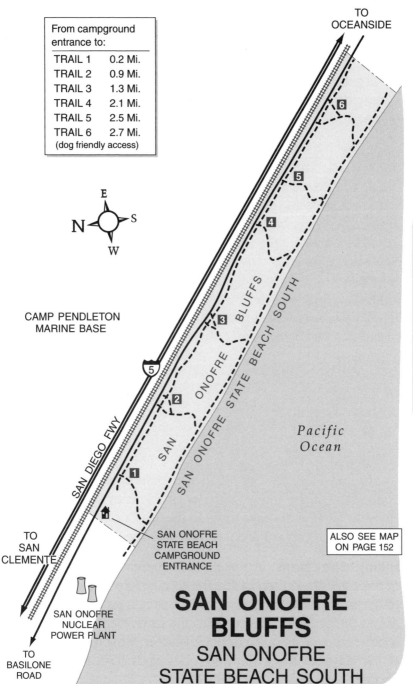

From campground entrance to:

TRAIL 1	0.2 Mi.
TRAIL 2	0.9 Mi.
TRAIL 3	1.3 Mi.
TRAIL 4	2.1 Mi.
TRAIL 5	2.5 Mi.
TRAIL 6	2.7 Mi.
(dog friendly access)	

TO OCEANSIDE

N E S W

CAMP PENDLETON MARINE BASE

5

SAN DIEGO FWY

SAN ONOFRE STATE BEACH SOUTH

BLUFFS

SAN ONOFRE STATE BEACH

SAN ONOFRE

SAN DIEGO COUNTY

Pacific Ocean

TO SAN CLEMENTE

SAN ONOFRE STATE BEACH CAMPGROUND ENTRANCE

ALSO SEE MAP ON PAGE 152

SAN ONOFRE NUCLEAR POWER PLANT

TO BASILONE ROAD

SAN ONOFRE BLUFFS
SAN ONOFRE STATE BEACH SOUTH

Hike 69
North Carlsbad State Beach

Hiking distance: 1.5 miles round trip
Hiking time: 1 hour
Elevation gain: Level
Maps: U.S.G.S. San Luis Rey

Summary of hike: Carlsbad State Beach is a sand and rock beach bordered by 40-foot bluffs. At the north end of the beach is a paved walking path on the bluffs along Carlsbad Boulevard, between Tamarack Avenue and Pine Avenue. Beneath the bluffs, a wide, parallel path, known as the Seawall Walkway, follows the beach strand. The two walkways are connected by numerous stairways and ramps. At the south end of the walking paths is Agua Hedionda Lagoon, a 400-acre tidal estuary with freshwater and saltwater marshes. The wetland is part of the Pacific Flyway, a feeding, nesting, and resting habitat for shorebirds and waterfowl.

Driving directions: From I-5 (San Diego Freeway) in Carlsbad, take the Tamarack Avenue exit, and head 0.6 miles west to Carlsbad Boulevard at the oceanfront. Cross Carlsbad Boulevard, and park in the lot at the end of Tamarack Avenue.

Hiking directions: To begin, detour a short distance south to explore the rock jetty bordering the mouth of Agua Hedionda Lagoon. Return and head north on the paved blufftop path to Tamarack Avenue. Continue north atop the landscaped bluffs or on the seawall path below. The sea level path follows the oceanfront, tucked between the hillside bluffs and the sandy beach. Several stairways connect the two paths. At Pine Avenue, the lower path slopes uphill to join the blufftop path. Return along either of the parallel paths.

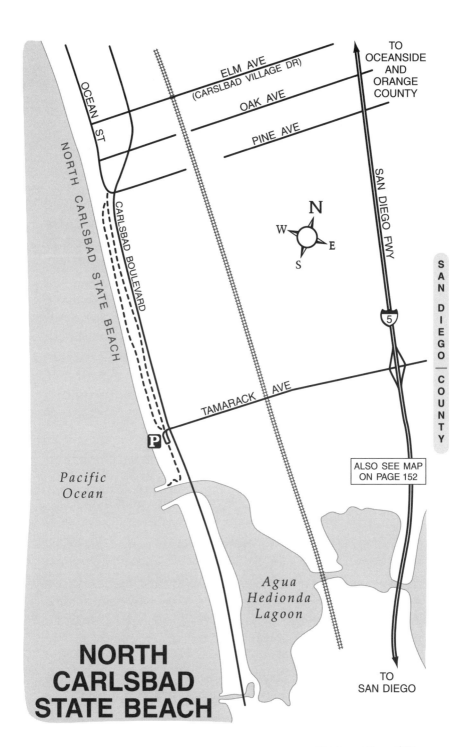

NORTH
CARLSBAD
STATE BEACH

Hike 70
North Shore Trail
BATIQUITOS LAGOON ECOLOGICAL RESERVE

Hiking distance: 3 miles round trip
Hiking time: 1.5 hours
Elevation gain: 40 feet
Maps: U.S.G.S. Encinitas

Summary of hike: Batiquitos Lagoon is a 600-acre wetland fed by Encinitas Creek, San Marcos Creek, and tidal flows. The lagoon rests in South Carlsbad, bordering the north edge of Leucadia. The coastal preserve serves as a sanctuary for rare, threatened, and endangered birds, animals, and plants. It is also a migratory waterfowl habitat with saltwater marshes, mudflats, salt flats, palms, eucalyptus trees, and native sage scrub vegetation. This wide trail follows the tranquil northern shoreline of the lagoon, beginning just east of I-5, and heads east to the inland end of the lagoon by El Camino Real. The western portion of the path is an 18-station interpretive trail with an accompanying pamphlet, available at the trailhead nature center.

Driving directions: From I-5 (San Diego Freeway) in Carlsbad, take the Poinsettia Lane exit, and head 0.4 miles east to Batiquitos Drive. Turn right and drive 0.5 miles to Gabriano Lane. Turn right and continue 0.3 miles to the parking lot at the end of the road.

Hiking directions: Take the wide, paved path east, curving away from I-5. Pass the nature center on the left. Follow the unpaved path past the interpretive panels along the north edge of Batiquitos Lagoon. At signpost 3 is a westward view of the three bridges spanning the lagoon by way of I-5, the railroad tracks, and Carlsbad Boulevard. Continue east between the sandstone cliffs and the lagoon. At signpost 8, by Indian shell fragments, a path leads up the forested hillside to Batiquitos Drive. The main trail stays on the edge of the lagoon, passing castor bean plants, coastal sage, palms, eucalyptus trees, mudflats, marshland, and the lush riparian habitat. Curve around the wetland area, passing an access path to parking lot 2 on the left by signpost 18. At 1.5 miles, near a road gate, a path on the left leads up the bluffs to another parking lot on Batiquitos Drive. The shoreline trail continues another mile to El Camino Real at the east end of the lagoon. Return by retracing your steps.

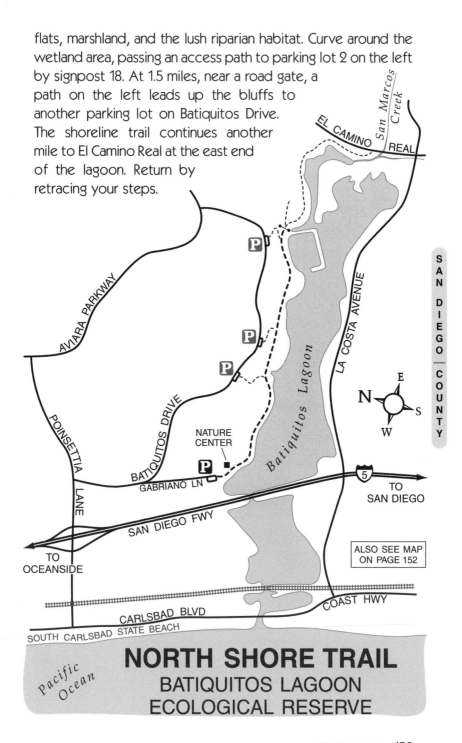

NORTH SHORE TRAIL
BATIQUITOS LAGOON
ECOLOGICAL RESERVE

Hike 71
Moonlight State Beach to Beacon's Beach

Hiking distance: 2.8 miles round trip
Hiking time: 1.5 hours
Elevation gain: 75 feet
Maps: U.S.G.S. Encinitas

Summary of hike: The hike from Moonlight State Beach to Beacon's Beach follows a 1.4-mile stretch of bluff-backed coastline. The beach strand lies between Encinitas Boulevard and Leucadia Boulevard in the town Leucadia, part of the city of Encinitas. Moonlight State Beach is a broad, crescent-shaped cove flanked with sandstone cliffs. Cottonwood Creek drains into the ocean through the sandy beach. It is a popular, easily accessible swimming, surfing, and picnicking beach with a blufftop overlook and benches. Beacon's Beach (formerly known as Leucadia State Beach) is a narrow, bluff-backed beach and a popular area for surfing and skin diving. A stairway and ramp zigzag down the eroding 80-foot cliffs to the beach strand below a viewing platform. Between these two beaches is Seaside Gardens County Park, locally called Stone Steps Beach, and Encinitas Beach, a secluded beach without direct access. Stone Steps Beach is a narrow, cobble beach reached from a long, partially stone stairway of 97 steps, dropping 80 feet down the eroding sandstone cliffs from Neptune Avenue. Encinitas Beach is accessed by either walking south from Beacon's Beach or north from Stone Steps Beach.

Driving directions: From I-5 (San Diego Freeway) in Encinitas, take the Encinitas Boulevard exit, and head 0.6 miles west to 3rd Street. Turn left one block to C Street and turn right. Park in the parking lot on the right, atop the hill overlooking the ocean.

Hiking directions: Take the ramped walkway on the right to the oceanfront at the west end of B Street. Cross the Cottonwood Creek drainage, and walk along the hard-packed sand beneath the 80-foot eroding sandstone cliffs. Homes line the cliff tops along this stretch of beach. At 0.6 miles, pass a lifeguard tower and a rock staircase to the blufftop at Stone Steps Beach (Seaside Gardens County Park). Continue north through Encinitas Beach County Park to a dirt path trail at Beacon's Beach. Wind up the cliffs to a blufftop parking lot and overlook. This is the turnaround spot. Return by retracing your route.

To make a loop, from the overlook on Neptune Avenue by Jasper Street, follow Neptune Avenue south through the residential neighborhood, curving onto Sylvia Street. Turn right on 4th Street, back to Moonlight Beach.

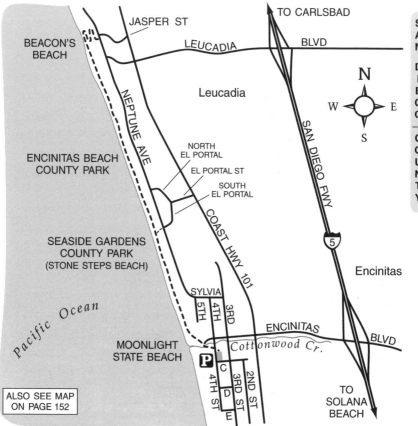

MOONLIGHT STATE BEACH
TO BEACON'S BEACH

Hike 72
Cardiff State Beach to San Elijo State Beach, Sea Cliff Park, and Swami's Beach

Hiking distance: 3.5 miles round trip
Hiking time: 2 hours
Elevation gain: 80 feet
Maps: U.S.G.S. Encinitas

Summary of hike: From Cardiff State Beach, at the mouth of San Elijo Lagoon, to Swami's Beach is a 1.7-mile stretch of cobblestone and sand beach backed by 80-foot jagged cliffs. San Elijo State Beach lies between, connecting the small coastal community of Cardiff-By-The-Sea with Encinitas. The state beach has a developed campground lining the bluffs. Wooden stairs lead from the campground to the shoreline. Swami's Beach is a popular surfing spot. Atop the bluffs at Swami's Beach is the Self-Realization Fellowship Hermitage Grounds, a 17-acre retreat founded in 1937 by Indian guru Paramahansa Yogananda. The cliffside meditation garden has flower-lined tiled pathways, tropical foliage, waterfalls, serene ponds with koi, and oceanfront overlooks. On the south side of the sanctuary is Sea Cliff Park (also known as Swami's Park), a blufftop park with a grassy picnic area and overlook. A long stairwell leads down the cliffs to Swami's Beach.

Driving directions: From I-5 (San Diego Freeway) in Encinitas, take the Manchester Avenue exit, and head 1.3 miles west to Chesterfield Drive. (En route, the road curves right and becomes San Elijo Avenue.) Turn left on Chesterfield and drive one block to the Coast Highway, crossing over the railroad tracks. Turn left and continue 0.4 miles, crossing over San Elijo Lagoon, to the Cardiff State Beach entrance. Park in the day-use lot on the right.

Hiking directions: From the north end of the parking lot, cross the Coast Highway bridge over the mouth of San Elijo Lagoon. After crossing, skirt the north bank of the lagoon to the oceanfront, along the edge of the San Elijo Campground. Curve around the sandstone cliffs, and follow the coastline between the cliffs and the sea. At 1 mile, a paved ramp switchbacks south up the cliffs to a parking lot on the Coast Highway. Continue below the plant-stabilized cliffs to Swami's Beach at 1.5 miles, where the cliffs curve out to sea. Atop the bluffs are three large lotus towers on the Hermitage Grounds. A steep stairway climbs the 80-foot, palm-lined cliffs to the parking lot on the bluffs at Sea Cliff (Swami's) Park. Walk one block north (left) on the Coast Highway to the Self-Realization Fellowship Hermitage, and quietly explore the magnificent grounds. To return, either retrace your steps or follow the walking path south along the Coast Highway, passing the San Elijo Campground to the trailhead.

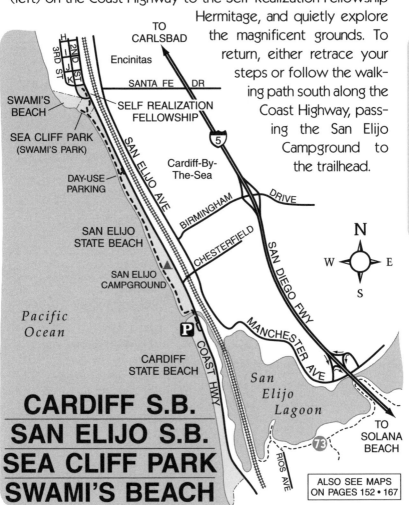

Hike 73
San Elijo Lagoon West Basin

Hiking distance: 3 miles round trip
Hiking time: 1.5 hours
Elevation gain: 125 feet
Maps: U.S.G.S. Encinitas

map
next page

Summary of hike: San Elijo Lagoon Ecological Reserve, stretching over a thousand acres, is a mixture of freshwater from Escondido and La Orilla Creeks and saltwater from the ocean. The estuary is a wildlife haven that supports large populations of migratory shorebirds and waterfowl. The wetland reserve has more than 7 miles of trails, making it easily accessible to hikers and birdwatchers. This hike begins on the south shore and follows the wetlands on the Gemma Parks Interpretive Trail. The shoreline path has informational panels about the lagoon's ecological history. A side path climbs up secluded Holmwood Canyon between eroded sandstone cliffs. Hikes 73 and 74 may be combined for a 6-mile hike.

Driving directions: From I-5 (San Diego Freeway) in Solana Beach, take the Lomas Santa Fe Drive exit, and head 0.8 miles west to Rios Avenue. Turn right and continue 0.8 miles to the posted trailhead at the end of the road.

Hiking directions: At the trailhead, on the south banks of San Elijo Lagoon, is a junction. Head west (left), overlooking the lagoon and the Pacific Ocean. Curve left and pass a footpath on the right that descends to the shoreline. The main trail loops around the hillside, dropping down to the lagoon by the railroad tracks. Parallel the tracks north to the trail's end. Return to the trailhead junction and head east. Drop down the north-facing cliffs past stands of castor bean trees to the edge of the lagoon on the interpretive path, which names the trees and plants. A half mile from the trailhead is a junction with the Gemma Parks Interpretive Trail on the left. This path hugs a water channel, then rejoins the main trail ahead. The main trail traverses the hillside to another junction. From the main trail, detour to the right and climb up narrow Holmwood Canyon under a grove of eucalyptus trees. The trail ends in a neighborhood on Holmwood Lane. Return to the lagoon and continue east. The Gemma Parks Interpretive Trail rejoins the main path below I-5. Curve left, parallel I-5 to the water channel, and cross under I-5. Curve right and wind through the open space to a junction. The left fork crosses a dike over the lagoon to Manchester Avenue. The right fork continues east to El Camino Real (Hike 74). Return along the same route.

Hike 74
San Elijo Lagoon East Basin
Tern Point and La Orilla Trail

Hiking distance: 3.5 miles round trip
Hiking time: 1.5 hours
Elevation gain: 90 feet
Maps: U.S.G.S. Encinitas and Rancho Santa Fe

map next page

Summary of hike: San Elijo Lagoon Ecological Reserve is one of San Diego County's largest remaining coastal wetlands, encompassing more than a thousand acres. The brackish lagoon is located in Solana Beach and empties into the Pacific Ocean. The wetland reserve has over 7 miles of trails through chaparral and marshland, with 8 separate trailheads. This hike begins on the south shore and follows the wetlands east to Tern Point, an overlook of the lagoon. It continues on the La Orilla Trail through a lush, shaded woodland.

Driving directions: From I-5 (San Diego Freeway) in Solana Beach, take the Lomas Santa Fe Drive exit, and head one block east to Santa Helena. Turn left and drive 0.5 miles to Santa Victoria. Turn left and continue 0.2 miles to Santa Carina. Turn left and go 0.2 miles. Park at the end of the road.

Hiking directions: From the north end of Santa Carina, gently descend through the sagebrush to the eucalyptus grove.

Bear left on one of several distinct paths that lead west towards I-5. The upper trail leads to Tern Point, offering the best vista of the entire east lagoon basin and the ocean. From the point, continue west, dropping into the lowlands where all the paths merge. Skirt the south edge of the lagoon beneath the 100-foot hillside to a junction. The right fork crosses a dike over the lagoon to Manchester Avenue. The left fork loops under I-5 to the west half of San Elijo Lagoon (Hike 73). Return to Tern Point and head east to the prominent eucalyptus grove. Descend through tall foliage and scattered Torrey pines. Cross under power poles and continue east. The last quarter mile winds through a lush, shaded grove of sycamores, bays, and eucalyptus trees fed by La Orilla Creek. The path ends on El Camino Real just south of the creek. Return along the same trail.

HIKES 73 • 74
SAN ELIJO LAGOON
WEST BASIN–EAST BASIN

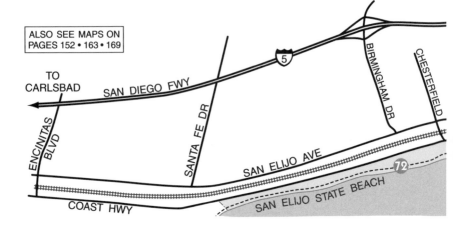

ALSO SEE MAPS ON
PAGES 152 • 163 • 169

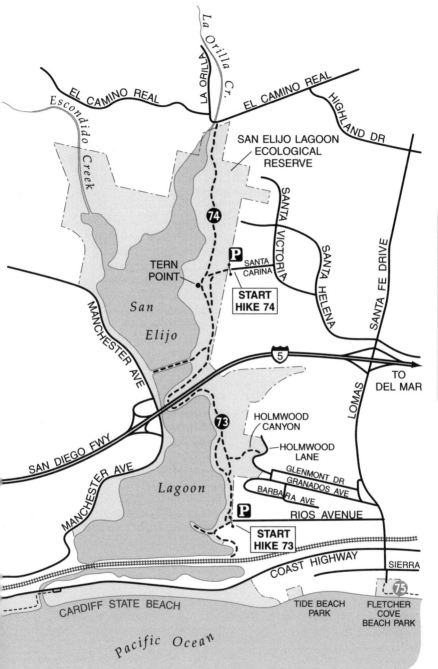

La Orilla Cr.

EL CAMINO REAL

Escondido Creek

EL CAMINO REAL

HIGHLAND DR

SAN ELIJO LAGOON
ECOLOGICAL
RESERVE

SANTA VICTORIA

SANTA HELENA

SANTA FE DRIVE

74

P SANTA
CARINA

TERN
POINT

**START
HIKE 74**

San

Elijo

MANCHESTER AVE

5

TO
DEL MAR

LOMAS

HOLMWOOD
CANYON

73

SAN DIEGO FWY

HOLMWOOD
LANE

GLENMONT DR

GRANADOS AVE

BARBARA AVE

Lagoon

MANCHESTER AVE

P

RIOS AVENUE

**START
HIKE 73**

SIERRA

75

COAST HIGHWAY

CARDIFF STATE BEACH

TIDE BEACH
PARK

FLETCHER
COVE
BEACH PARK

Pacific Ocean

SAN DIEGO COUNTY

Hike 75
Fletcher Cove to
Dog Beach and Scripps Bluff Preserve

Hiking distance: 2.5 miles round trip
Hiking time: 1.5 hours
Elevation gain: 80 feet
Maps: U.S.G.S. Del Mar

Summary of hike: Tide Beach Park, Fletcher Cove Beach Park, North Seascape Surf Beach Park, and Del Mar Shores Beach Park are all part of Solana Beach. The cliff-lined sandy beach strand stretches for 1.8 miles from the San Elijo Lagoon to the San Dieguito Lagoon. This hike begins at Fletcher Cove on a grassy blufftop overlooking the sandy recess, also known as Pill Box Beach. The hike heads south along the coast to Del Mar Shores Beach Park, called Dog Beach because dogs are allowed off-leash freedom. Dog Beach is a wide, sandy beach at the mouth of the San Dieguito Lagoon on the northern end of Del Mar. A steep, wooden staircase leads up to Scripps Bluff Preserve on 80-foot bluffs overlooking Dog Beach and the San Dieguito Lagoon.

Driving directions: From I-5 (San Diego Freeway) in Solana Beach, take the Lomas Santa Fe Drive exit, and head 1 mile west to the west end of Lomas Santa Fe Drive at Sierra Avenue, just past the Coast Highway. Continue one block straight ahead on Plaza Street to Fletcher Cove Park.

Hiking directions: Begin at the grassy ocean overlook in Fletcher Cove Park. Walk down the paved ramp to the shoreline below the cliff top park. Head south beneath the eroding sandstone cliffs. At 0.6 miles, the cliffs jut 50 yards out to sea, and a concrete stairway climbs the cliffs to the Seascape Surf Beach access on Sierra Avenue by Del Mar Shores Terrace. Continue along the coastline, passing a hillside retaining wall as the multi-colored cliffs become more dramatic and chiseled. Stroll along a 4-foot high rock shelf that is embedded with seashells and a great display of tidepools. The cliffs descend near Dog Beach at the mouth of the San Dieguito River in Del Mar. Curve left, following the edge of the cliffs to the access steps for the James G. Scripps Bluff Preserve. Climb the wood stairs up the cliffs. At the mesa, a path leads to the edge of the 80-foot bluffs, with sweeping panoramas of the San Dieguito River Basin, Del Mar Race Track, and the Pacific Ocean.

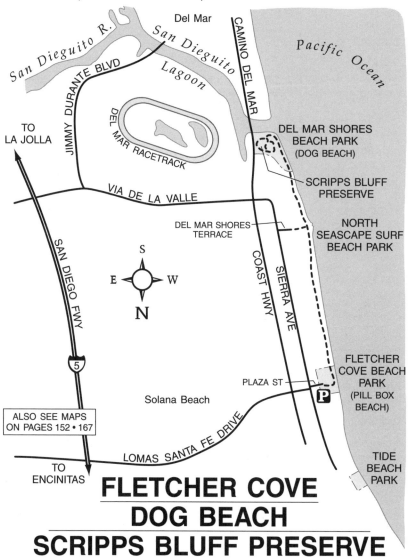

FLETCHER COVE
DOG BEACH
SCRIPPS BLUFF PRESERVE

Hike 76
Torrey Pines State Beach
to Seagrove and Powerhouse Parks

Hiking distance: 3.8 miles round trip
Hiking time: 2 hours
Elevation gain: 100 feet
Maps: U.S.G.S. Del Mar

Summary of hike: Torrey Pines State Beach is a wide, sandy beach backed by sandstone bluffs. The state beach extends 4.5 miles, from 6th Street in the city of Del Mar to Torrey Pines City Beach north of La Jolla. The beach is divided by Los Penasquitos Creek, a 385-acre saltwater estuary. The wetlands serve as a bird sanctuary and wildlife refuge. To the north, within Del Mar City Beach, is Seagrove and Powerhouse Parks, two adjacent oceanfront parks with paved paths. Seagrove Park is dotted with Torrey pines on a 60-foot tall bluff overlooking the ocean. This hike follows the north portion of Torrey Pines State Beach, from the mouth of Los Penasquitos Lagoon to Seagrove and Powerhouse Parks.

Driving directions: From I-5 (San Diego Freeway) in Torrey Pines, take the Carmel Valley Road exit, and head 1.1 miles west to McGonigle Road. Turn left and continue 0.1 mile to the parking lot on the north edge of Los Penasquitos Marsh Natural Preserve.

Hiking directions: Follow the paved path under Camino Del Mar to the oceanfront on the north side of Los Penasquitos Marsh. To the south is Torrey Pines State Reserve (Hikes 77—81). Head north as the sandstone cliffs quickly rise 100 feet, with railroad tracks perched halfway up the cliffs. Pass flat slab rocks with tidepools as the cliffs drop down to a sandy beachfront at Powerhouse Park. Walk up to the park, and curve right (south) on the blufftop path into the landscaped gardens of Seagrove Park. Cross the railroad tracks and follow the blufftop path south. Pass steep surfer paths down the cliffs, and continue past beach accesses at 9th, 8th, 7th, and 4th Streets. The trail descends the bluffs, returning to the Los Penasquitos Lagoon.

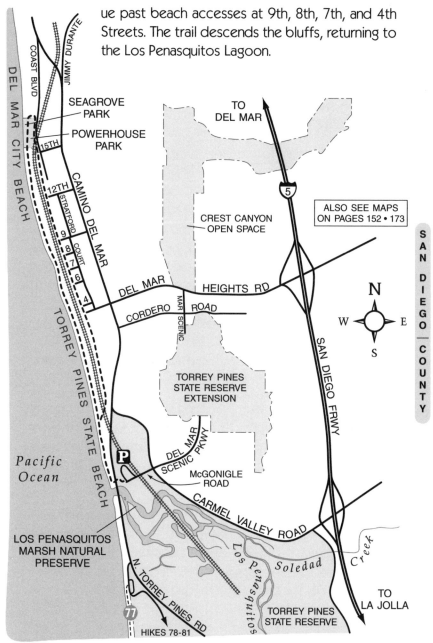

ALSO SEE MAPS ON PAGES 152 • 173

TORREY PINES STATE BEACH
TO SEAGROVE and POWERHOUSE PARKS

Hike 77
Torrey Pines State Beach • Flat Rock

Hiking distance: 2.6 mile loop
Hiking time: 1.5 hours
Elevation gain: 350 feet
Maps: U.S.G.S. Del Mar

Summary of hike: Torrey Pines State Beach is a wide sandy beach backed by dramatic 300-foot sandstone bluffs, some of the tallest coastal cliffs in San Diego County. The beach is located between Del Mar and La Jolla beneath the wild, weather-beaten cliffs of Torrey Pines State Reserve. The hike follows the isolated southern portion of the state beach, passing deep badland canyons and razor-edged ridges dotted with Torrey pines. The beach continues to the tidepools at Flat Rock, an erosion-resistant slab rock protruding out to sea. The return route climbs the sculpted sedimentary cliffs to the bluffs and loops back on the descending park road.
CAUTION: This beach cannot be hiked at high tide. Check a tide table or with the park rangers before setting out.

Driving directions: From I-5 (San Diego Freeway) in Torrey Pines, take the Carmel Valley Road exit, and head 1.5 miles west to Camino Del Mar. Turn left and drive 0.8 miles to the Torrey Pines State Reserve entrance on the right. Pass the entrance kiosk and park in the lot on the left.

Hiking directions: Walk down to the oceanfront, and bear left along the base of the imposing 300-foot cliffs. Pass a series of water-carved badland gorges, including the out-of-this-world, moonscape-like gorge separating Razor Point and Yucca Point. At 1 mile, the path reaches Flat Rock, a large, offshore slab rock and popular sitting spot. After enjoying the shoreline, ascend the steps to an upper shelf and trail junction. The Broken Hill Trail (to the right) zippers up the sloping hillside to the park road. Instead, take the left fork on the Beach Trail and wind up the hillside, passing the Yucca Point and Razor Point Trails (Hike

80), both on the left. Stay to the right on the Beach Trail, passing the south edge of Red Butte, to the park road across from the visitor center and ranger station at 1.7 miles. Descend along the paved park road to the left, a popular walking and jogging route. Wind 0.9 miles downhill to the trailhead parking lot at the base of the mountain, passing the High Point Trail on the right, the Parry Grove Trail on the left (Hike 79), and the North Grove—Guy Fleming Loop on the left (Hike 78).

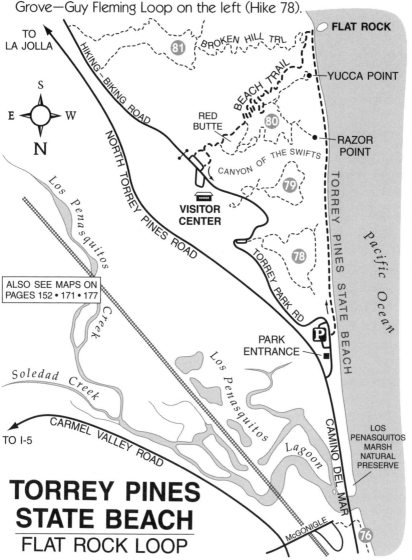

TORREY PINES
STATE BEACH
FLAT ROCK LOOP

Torrey Pines State Reserve
HIKES 78—81

Torrey Pines State Reserve is one of the premier coastal preserves in the California state park system and one of the best hiking destinations in San Diego County (cover photo). The magnificent 1,700-acre natural reserve is located between Del Mar and La Jolla. The area includes five miles of pristine beach; the Los Penasquitos Lagoon; precipitous, weather-beaten cliffs and bluffs; bold oceanfront headlands with a series of narrow, eroding ridges; deep, rugged gorges with sculpted badland formations; and a 350-foot marine terrace with coastal sage scrub and upland chaparral plant communities.

Highlighting the reserve's many magnificent features is its namesake, the twisted, weathered Torrey pines. The primeval Torrey pine, a relic of the Ice Age (over 11,000 years), is the rarest pine tree in America and among the rarest in the world. The unique maritime pines are indigenous to the small area within the coastal community of Del Mar and to Santa Rosa Island, one of the Channel Islands off the Santa Barbara coast. Scattered groves of the gnarled, wind-sculpted trees grace the bluffs and cling to the picturesque cliffs.

The state reserve visitor center is located in an old pueblo-style adobe structure built in 1923, surrounded by native plant gardens. The center has natural and cultural history exhibits, interactive displays, and a small gift shop.

A network of maintained hiking trails traverses through the state reserve. Some trails cross the ancient cliffs through native chaparral and stands of scraggly Torrey pines to aeries at the tip of 350-foot sandstone ridges. Other paths descend the rolling coastal terrace through steep-sided gullies with colorful sandstone, traversing down sculpted flutes and scarps to the isolated stretch of coastline. The footpaths offer great views of the Pacific Ocean, San Clemente Island, Catalina Island, Los Penasquitos Marsh, the inland hills, and the coastal towns of Del Mar and La Jolla.

Driving directions: From I-5 (San Diego Freeway) in Torrey Pines, take the Carmel Valley Road exit, and head 1.5 miles west to Camino Del Mar. Turn left and drive 0.8 miles to the Torrey Pines State Reserve entrance. Pass the park entrance station, and drive 0.9 miles to the visitor center/ranger station parking lot on the left. A parking fee is required.

Hike 78
Guy Fleming Trail • North Grove
TORREY PINES STATE RESERVE

Hiking distance: 1.5 miles round trip (from visitor center)
Hiking time: 1 hour
Elevation gain: 60 feet
Maps: U.S.G.S. Del Mar

map next page

SAN DIEGO COUNTY

Summary of hike: The Guy Fleming Trail is an easy 0.7-mile interpretive loop around North Grove, a dense stand of twisted Torrey pines. The trail is named in honor of the late conservationist, naturalist, and park supervisor. The diverse trail contours the windswept mesa past sandstone formations, continuing to two coastal overlooks perched 250 feet above the sea. The North Overlook offers views of Torrey Pines State Beach, the Los Penasquitos Marsh, and the city of Del Mar. The South Overlook vistas extend to Scripps Pier, La Jolla Bay, the city of La Jolla, San Clemente Island, and Catalina Island.

Driving directions: From I-5 (San Diego Freeway) in Torrey Pines, take the Carmel Valley Road exit, and head 1.5 miles west to Camino Del Mar. Turn left and drive 0.8 miles to the Torrey Pines State Reserve entrance. Pass the park entrance station, and drive 0.9 miles to the visitor center/ranger station parking lot on the left. A parking fee is required. There is also a parking pullout on the right, just before the actual trailhead, located 0.5 miles from the park entrance station.

Hiking directions: Walk back down the park road 0.4 miles, passing the Whitaker Garden—Parry Grove Trail (Hike 79) on the left, to the posted North Grove—Guy Fleming Trail, also on the left. Take the footpath 20 yards to the beginning of the loop. Bear right, curving around a sandstone formation on the left.

Continue northwest through a grove of Torrey pines, with views of Los Penasquitos Lagoon and the inland hills. The path, carpeted with pine needles, curves left to the oceanfront. Pass gnarled, windswept Torrey pines to North Overlook, a coastal vista point. Head south along the edge of the coastal cliffs, and curve inland to a side path. Detour to the right to South Overlook, with a viewing platform extending from the cliffs. Return to the Guy Fleming Trail and complete the loop. Bear right, back to the park road.

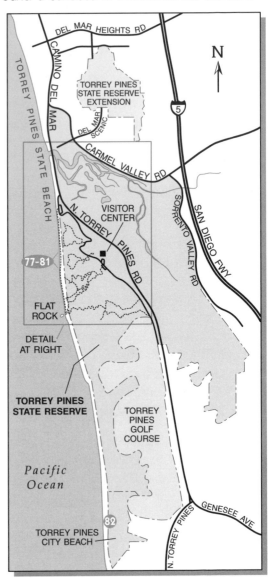

HIKES 78–81
TORREY PINES STATE RESERVE

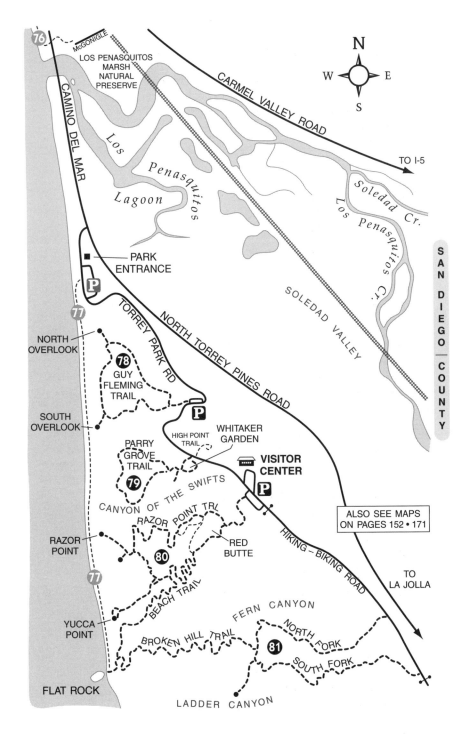

N
W E
S

76
McGONIGLE
LOS PENASQUITOS
MARSH
NATURAL
PRESERVE

CARMEL VALLEY ROAD

TO I-5

Los

Penasquitos

Lagoon

Soledad Cr.

Los Penasquitos Cr.

CAMINO DEL MAR

PARK
ENTRANCE

P

77

NORTH
OVERLOOK

78
GUY
FLEMING
TRAIL

TORREY PARK RD

NORTH TORREY PINES ROAD

SOLEDAD VALLEY

SAN DIEGO COUNTY

SOUTH
OVERLOOK

P

HIGH POINT
TRAIL

WHITAKER
GARDEN

PARRY
GROVE
TRAIL

79

VISITOR
CENTER

P

CANYON OF THE SWIFTS

RAZOR POINT TRL

ALSO SEE MAPS
ON PAGES 152 • 171

RAZOR
POINT

80

RED
BUTTE

HIKING – BIKING ROAD

TO
LA JOLLA

YUCCA
POINT

BEACH TRAIL

BROKEN HILL TRAIL

FERN CANYON

NORTH FORK

81

SOUTH FORK

77

FLAT ROCK

LADDER CANYON

Hike 79
Parry Grove Trail • Whitaker Garden
TORREY PINES STATE RESERVE

Hiking distance: 0.8 miles round trip (from visitor center)
Hiking time: 30 minutes
Elevation gain: 100 feet
Maps: U.S.G.S. Del Mar

map page 177

Summary of hike: The Parry Grove Trail is a half-mile loop named for the botanist who originally described and named the Torrey pine. The steep path descends 100 steps to the oldest grove of Torrey pines in the state reserve, dating back to the 1870s. The trail contours the oceanfront slope and includes sitting benches that overlook the Canyon of the Swifts, a deep and rugged gorge. The trail begins at the Whitaker Memorial Native Plant Garden, a garden with labeled native California plants that can be seen throughout the park.

Driving directions: From I-5 (San Diego Freeway) in Torrey Pines, take the Carmel Valley Road exit, and head 1.5 miles west to Camino Del Mar. Turn left and drive 0.8 miles to the Torrey Pines State Reserve entrance. Pass the park entrance station, and drive 0.9 miles to the visitor center/ranger station parking lot on the left. A parking fee is required.

Hiking directions: Walk back down the park road 0.1 mile to the posted Parry Grove Trail on the left. Enter the small but charming Whitaker Garden, an interpretive garden with native California plants. Walk through the garden to the beginning of the Parry Grove Trail. Bear right and descend 100 steps from the bluffs into the northern ravine and a posted junction. Begin the loop to the right, strolling through sage scrub, chaparral, cactus, and scattered Torrey pines. Loop around the coastal bluffs. The vistas span across the canyons to the narrow ridges of Razor Point and Yucca Point, Scripps Pier, and the coastal community of La Jolla. Return along the north edge of the Canyon of the Swifts, overlooking carved sandstone formations with caves.

Complete the loop and return up the cliffs on the steep steps to Whitaker Garden.

Hike 80
Razor Point—Yucca Point—Beach Trail Loop
TORREY PINES STATE RESERVE

Hiking distance: 2 mile loop
Hiking time: 1 hour
Elevation gain: 350 feet
Maps: U.S.G.S. Del Mar

map
page 177

Summary of hike: The Beach Trail links the rolling coastal bluffs to the isolated beach at Flat Rock. The trail winds through a dramatic, weather-sculpted drainage to the remote, sandy beach pocket with tidepools and offshore rocks. This hike also includes Razor Point and Yucca Point, two overlooks on narrow, west-facing ridge tips that overlook the ocean and coastline. The precipitous views include the eroded sandstone canyons (cover photo), Flat and Mussel Rocks, Scripps Pier, Hang Glider Point, and the city of La Jolla.

Driving directions: From I-5 (San Diego Freeway) in Torrey Pines, take the Carmel Valley Road exit, and head 1.5 miles west to Camino Del Mar. Turn left and drive 0.8 miles to the Torrey Pines State Reserve entrance. Pass the park entrance station, and drive 0.9 miles to the visitor center/ranger station parking lot on the left. A parking fee is required.

Hiking directions: From the visitor center, walk across the park road to the trailhead and information board. Head west towards Red Butte, the prominent sandstone formation, to a posted junction. To the left is the Beach Trail, our return route. Bear right on the Razor Point Trail, and wind uphill to the Red Butte summit and an overlook. Take the right fork downhill along the south edge of a deep gorge with sculpted formations, overlooking the scalloped coastal cliffs and ocean. The serpentine path continues west to a junction with the Beach Trail.

For now, stay to the right along the eroding, deeply etched cliffs. The path ends at a wooden platform on the 300-foot ridge tip of Razor Point. Return to the junction with the Beach Trail and go to the right, crossing the head of a deep, eroded canyon to a junction. Detour to the right to Yucca Point on another narrow, finger ridge on the edge of Canyon of the Swifts. Pass Mojave and whipple yucca plants to the west end of the 300-foot ridge. A small loop circles the point, with great views of the beach at Flat Rock and the La Jolla headland. Return to the Beach Trail and bear right. Zigzag down the draw to a junction with the Broken Hill Trail on the left (Hike 81). Scramble down the last stretch, dropping over a small ledge to the beach at Flat Rock. The large, offshore slab rock is a popular spot for sitting and observing the surf. To return, head back up the draw to the Beach—Yucca Trail junction. Stay to the right on the Beach Trail, winding up the hillside and returning to the trailhead.

For a loop hike that includes the state beach, see Hike 77.

Hike 81
Broken Hill Trail to Flat Rock
TORREY PINES STATE RESERVE

Hiking distance: 3.3 miles round trip
Hiking time: 2 hours
Elevation gain: 350 feet
Maps: U.S.G.S. Del Mar

map
page 177

Summary of hike: The Broken Hill Trails are the longest trails in Torrey Pines State Park. The North and South Forks form a loop, then join and head down to the beach at Flat Rock. Both trails cross the rolling, chaparral-covered coastal bluffs along the drier section of the reserve. A short detour leads to the Broken Hill Overlook, a 300-foot escarpment with a view into the desert-looking badlands of Ladder Canyon. From the 350-foot terrace, the trail zigzags through a deep sandstone ravine to the sandy beach pocket with offshore rocks, tidepools, and Flat Rock.

Driving directions: From I-5 (San Diego Freeway) in Torrey Pines, take the Carmel Valley Road exit, and head 1.5 miles west to Camino Del Mar. Turn left and drive 0.8 miles to the Torrey Pines State Reserve entrance. Pass the park entrance station, and drive 0.9 miles to the visitor center/ranger station parking lot on the left. A parking fee is required.

Hiking directions: From the visitor center, take the vehicle-restricted park road southeast (the old highway between San Diego and Los Angeles). The road follows the 400-foot ridge above the Soledad Valley on the east and the Torrey Pines State Reserve and ocean on the west. Pass the posted North Fork Trail (our return route) at 0.3 miles. Continue to the South Fork Trail at a half mile. Head west on the footpath through the dense chaparral. The near-level trail curves right along the edge of the 300-foot bluffs, offering views of the magnificent cliffs, the lush green golf course, and the ocean. At just under a mile, the trail reaches a junction. Detour left to the Broken Hill Overlook, located on a sandstone fin with surrealistic views of the dramatic badlands. Return to the main trail, and continue 30 yards to another junction. Bear left on the Broken Hill Trail, zigzagging down the sloping hillside while overlooking the sea, Yucca Point, and the city of La Jolla. Near the point, curve right, merging with the Beach Trail coming in from the right (Hike 80). Descend steps and scramble down a ledge to the shoreline, just north of Flat Rock. The large, offshore slab rock is a popular spot for sitting and observing the surf. To return, head back up the Broken Hill Trail to the junction with the North Fork Trail. Continue to the left, winding along the flat hilltop that overlooks Fern Canyon. At the park road, return 0.3 miles back to the visitor center.

For a loop hike that includes the state beach, see Hike 77.

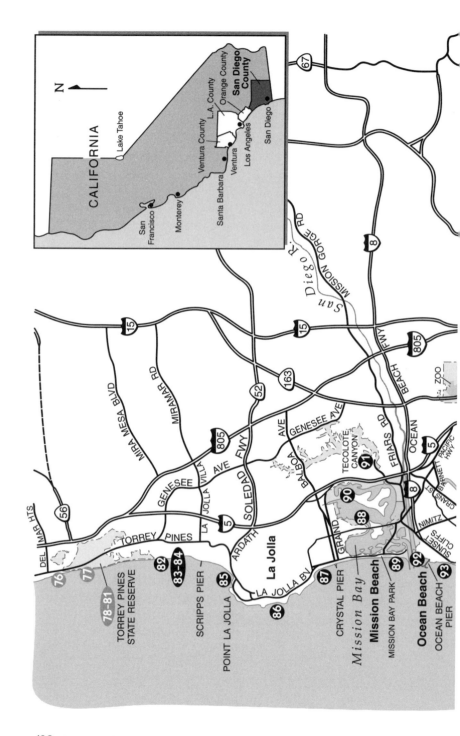

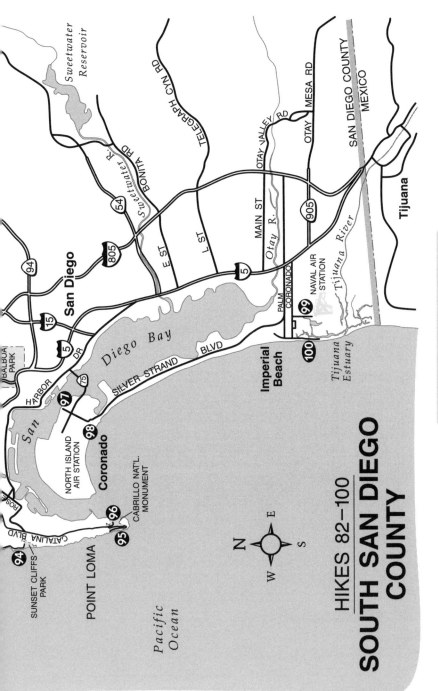

HIKES 82–100
SOUTH SAN DIEGO COUNTY

Sweetwater Reservoir

TELEGRAPH CYN RD

OTAY MESA RD

SAN DIEGO COUNTY
MEXICO

Tijuana

San Diego

94

805

BONITA RD

Sweetwater Rd

54

E ST

L ST

MAIN ST

OTAY VALLEY RD

Otay R.

905

NAVAL AIR STATION

Tijuana River

99

100

Tijuana Estuary

15

5

DR

Diego Bay

SILVER STRAND BLVD

PALM
CORONADO

Imperial Beach

75

HARBOR

97

San

98

NORTH ISLAND AIR STATION

Coronado

ROSE

CABRILLO NAT'L. MONUMENT

96

95

CATALINA BLVD

94

SUNSET CLIFFS PARK

POINT LOMA

Pacific Ocean

BALBOA PARK

N
W E S

Hike 82
Torrey Pines Glider Port Park
to Black's Beach

Hiking distance: 2 miles round trip
Hiking time: 1 hour
Elevation gain: 300 feet
Maps: U.S.G.S. Del Mar

map
next page

Summary of hike: Torrey Pines Glider Port Park lies within Torrey Pines City Park on 300-foot oceanfront sandstone bluffs, located between Del Mar and La Jolla at the south end of Torrey Pines State Reserve. The park towers above Torrey Pines City Beach, known locally as Black's Beach, a well-known clothing-optional beach. The barren bluffs overlook Scripps Pier and the scalloped coastline. The strong winds that strike the oceanfront bluffs create updrafts, making it an ideal and popular hang gliding and paragliding area. A steep, half-mile-long path leads down the weather-worn cliffs to Black's Beach.

Driving directions: From I-5 (San Diego Freeway) in Sorrento Valley, take the Genesee Avenue exit, and head 0.8 miles west to North Torrey Pines Road. Turn left and drive 0.4 miles to Torrey Pines Scenic Drive. Turn right and continue 0.4 miles to the historic Torrey Pines Glider Port entrance. Curve left to the oceanfront bluffs.

Hiking directions: Walk down the sloping blufftop to the majestic coastline views 300 feet above the sea. On the south side of the barren bluffs, descend the eroding cliffs, zigzagging on a manageable grade. Wind down a ravine with the aid of steps and handrails to the sandy beach beneath the towering cliffs. To the north is Torrey Pines State Beach (Hike 77). To the south, the beach leads to a rocky tidepool area by Scripps Pier and La Jolla Shores Beach by grassy Kellogg Park. After exploring, return to the blufftop. Walk 0.4 miles north to the north end of the parking area. A path follows the edge of the cliffs to northern vistas, including the multi-colored cliffs of Torrey

Pines State Reserve, the crenulated coastline, and the green grass of Torrey Pines Golf Course.

Hike 83
Black Canyon

Hiking distance: 3 miles round trip
Hiking time: 1.5 hours
Elevation gain: 350 feet
Maps: U.S.G.S. Del Mar and La Jolla

map
next page

Summary of hike: Black Canyon, at the north end of La Jolla, is one of the few undeveloped oceanfront canyons in San Diego County. The trail is a steep, vehicle-restricted road owned by the University of California that is a popular route for surfers, bikers, joggers, sunbathers, and hikers. From the multi-million dollar homes atop the mesa, the road winds a half mile down the 350-foot sandstone cliffs through the deep canyon to an unspoiled white-sand beach.

Driving directions: From I-5 (San Diego Freeway) near La Jolla, take the La Jolla Village Drive exit, and head 1.1 miles west to La Jolla Shores Drive. Turn left and quickly turn right onto La Jolla Farms Road. Continue 0.5 miles to the posted entrance on the left, across from Black Gold Road. Park alongside the curb in a strictly enforced 2-hour parking zone.

Hiking directions: The posted trailhead is on the west side of the road, directly across from Black Gold Road. Pass the trailhead gate and follow the paved road downhill on the north flank of Black Canyon. Drop deep into the canyon between the eroding sedimentary rock cliffs to an overlook with a V-shaped coastal view formed by the canyon walls. Make a sweeping S-curve between the towering sandstone walls. Near the bottom is a parking area for the UCSD Surfing Team. Curve around the parking area from left to right, reaching the sandy beach beneath the monolithic 350-foot cliffs. To the north is Black's Beach (Torrey Pines City Beach), an unofficial clothing-optional beach (Hike 82). To the south is a house extending off the cliffs 25 feet above the beach, with a private funicular tram to the mesa top. Beyond the house are tidepools; the 1,090-foot long Scripps Pier; and sandy La Jolla Shores Beach, a wide strand with a paved walkway adjacent to grassy Kellogg Park. Return by retracing your steps.

Hike 84
Scripps Coastal Reserve Biodiversity Trail

Hiking distance: 0.7 mile loop
Hiking time: 30 minutes
Elevation gain: 40 feet
Maps: U.S.G.S. Del Mar and La Jolla

Summary of hike: Scripps Coastal Reserve Biodiversity Trail is located on the 350-foot oceanfront cliffs at the north end of La Jolla. The reserve is a 152-acre undeveloped blufftop mesa bordered by deep canyons. It also includes an 80-acre underwater preserve. The mesa is an archaeological village site inhabited by La Jollan Indians between 3,000 and 8,000 years ago and later by the Diegueno Indians (also known as the Kumeyaay). The natural area has become a protected habitat managed by the University of California's Natural Reserve System. A self-guided trail circles the grassy mesa between Black Canyon on the north (Hike 83) and Sumner Canyon on the south. A brochure, available at the trailhead, highlights the habitats and ecology of the natural reserve, including diverse plants (over 200 species), birds (88 species), and mammals (12 species). There is no beach access, but the mesa offers magnificent coastal vistas.

Driving directions: From I-5 (San Diego Freeway) near La Jolla, take the La Jolla Village Drive exit, and head 1.1 miles west to La Jolla Shores Drive. Turn left and quickly turn right onto La Jolla Farms Road. Continue 0.1 mile to the posted gate entrance on the left (on the south side of 9402 La Jolla Farms Road). Park along the curb in a strictly enforced 2-hour parking zone.

Hiking directions: Head past the trailhead gate to a sign-in box at the beginning of the loop. Begin to the right, hiking counter-clockwise. Stroll along the south edge of Black Canyon. On the cliffs, across Black Canyon, is a conspicuous, jaw-dropping mega-home. Follow the oceanfront cliffs south, with great views of La Jolla and Scripps Pier. Curve inland along the north edge of Sumner Canyon. At interpretive station #12, an outer loop follows the edge of the bluffs and reconnects with the self-guiding trail at station #17. Complete the loop a short distance ahead.

ALSO SEE MAPS ON
PAGES 176 • 182 • 188

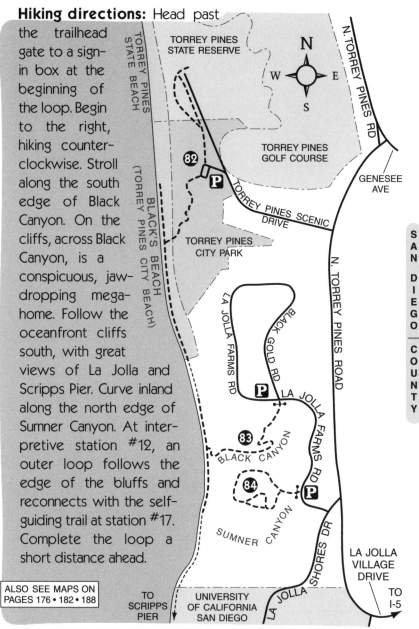

GLIDER PORT PARK • BLACK'S BEACH
BLACK CANYON
SCRIPPS COASTAL RESERVE

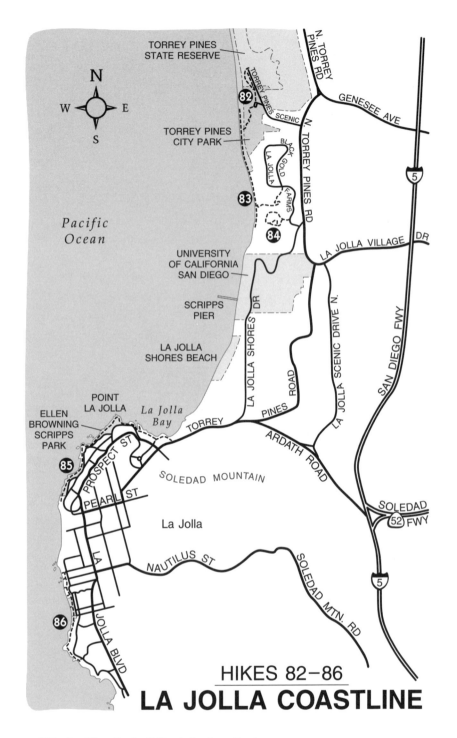

N

W   E

S

TORREY PINES
STATE RESERVE

N. TORREY PINES RD.

GENESEE AVE.

82

TORREY PINES
SCENIC

N. TORREY PINES RD.

TORREY PINES
CITY PARK

BLACK GOLD FARMS

LA JOLLA

83

84

*Pacific
Ocean*

LA JOLLA VILLAGE DR.

UNIVERSITY
OF CALIFORNIA
SAN DIEGO

5

SCRIPPS
PIER

LA JOLLA
SHORES BEACH

LA JOLLA SHORES DR.

LA JOLLA SCENIC DRIVE N.

SAN DIEGO FWY.

POINT
LA JOLLA

*La Jolla
Bay*

PINES ROAD

ELLEN
BROWNING
SCRIPPS
PARK

PROSPECT ST.

TORREY

ARDATH ROAD

85

PEARL ST.

SOLEDAD MOUNTAIN

SOLEDAD
52 FWY

La Jolla

NAUTILUS ST.

LA

5

SOLEDAD MTN. RD.

86

JOLLA BLVD.

HIKES 82–86
LA JOLLA COASTLINE

La Jolla Oceanfront
HIKES 85–86

La Jolla is an upscale resort town sitting on a terraced peninsula at the foot of Soledad Mountain, just 14 miles north of downtown San Diego. The peninsula juts out to sea with seven miles of curving picturesque coastline that is interspersed with jagged cliffs and coves. It is one of the most beautiful areas on the California coast. The scenic highlight of La Jolla is around Point La Jolla, surrounded by Ellen Browning Scripps Park and La Jolla Cove. The large grassy park has shade trees, picnic areas, and a paved bluff-edge path. La Jolla Cove is a small crescent-shaped beach pocket tucked between sculpted sandstone cliffs, riddled with tidepools and caves. Stairways connect the bluffs to the beach. The spectacular scenery also includes Seal Rock, an offshore rock with seals and sea lions; San Diego-La Jolla Underwater Park, an offshore ecological preserve comprised of nearly 6,000 acres of submerged reefs and tidal lands (popular for scuba diving and snorkeling); Point La Jolla extending seaward with a 40-foot escarpment; Goldfish Point, a promontory with groves of Torrey pines and a bird preserve; and the La Jolla Caves, a series of grottos and seven wave-carved caves in the sandstone cliffs.

S A N D I E G O C O U N T Y

Hike 85
La Jolla Bay to Nicholson Point

Hiking distance: 3 mile loop
Hiking time: 1.5 hours
Elevation gain: 30 feet
Maps: U.S.G.S. La Jolla

map
page 193

Summary of hike: This hike begins near La Jolla Bay on the terrace by the La Jolla Caves. The first part of the hike follows the Coast Walk, a blufftop dirt trail with bridges and stairways that curve around the perimeter of the alluvial 100-foot cliffs. The cliff-hugging path offers sweeping views of the ocean, beach, and caves. En route from the La Jolla Caves, the hike explores an array of small beaches tucked between folds of sandstone bluffs, eroded cliffs carved into ledges with roosting seabirds, sculpted caves, grottos, pocket beach coves, tidepools, and grassy blufftop parks. The path continues to Nicholson Point Park, a sandy cove at the base of the cliffs.

Driving directions: NORTHBOUND: From I-5 (San Diego Freeway) near La Jolla, take the Ardath Road exit, and head 2.5 miles west to Prospect Place. (Ardath Road merges onto Torrey Pines Road en route.) Turn right on Prospect Place, and search for a parking spot. A parking area for 5 cars is on the right, across from Park Row.

SOUTHBOUND: From I-5 (San Diego Freeway) near La Jolla, take the La Jolla Village Drive exit, and head 1.6 miles west to Torrey Pines Road. Turn left and drive 2.7 miles to Prospect Place. Turn right and search for a parking spot.

Hiking directions: The Coast Walk, an oceanfront blufftop path, can be accessed from many points. This hike begins on Prospect Place across from Park Row. Descend steps to the jagged cliffs and a vista of La Jolla Bay and Goldfish Point. Head to the right on the natural path, with wooden bridges and stairs that line the eroding cliffs of La Jolla Bay. The path ends at Torrey Pines Road. Return and head west to Goldfish Point. Take the steps to the right down the sloping finger of land to an overlook of the bird preserve on the point. Continue on the Coast Walk to Coast Boulevard. Follow the sidewalk to the right to a large cave on the west face of the Goldfish Point cliffs. Round the point to La Jolla Cove. A flat sandstone rock slab sits within the cove with caves and roosting pelicans. Follow the paved blufftop path, curving around the cove and passing stairs that lead down to the sandy beach. Loop around Point La Jolla, where additional steps lead down to the tidepool-filled rock slabs extending seaward. The boardwalk hugs the edge of the bluffs around the periphery of the grassy, tree-dotted Ellen Browning Scripps Park to Rocky Point at the south end of the park. Side paths lead down to Boomer Beach, a famous body surfing beach, and to Shell Beach. Leave the park and continue along the 50-foot cliffs overlooking Seal Rock. Children's Pool Beach sits at the base, an enclosed beach protected by a curving seawall. A walkway atop the breakwater leads out to sea for a close-up view of the seals and sea lions. Continue south, passing Seal Rock Point. Stroll through Coast Boulevard Park, with picnic areas and stairways to the beach. Curve around Whale View Point to the sandy cove of Nicholson Point, our turnaround spot. To return, retrace your steps or stroll through the village and upscale shops on Prospect Street.

Hike 86
South La Jolla Coastal Bluffs

Hiking distance: 1.6 miles round trip
Hiking time: 1 hour
Elevation gain: 20 feet
Maps: U.S.G.S. La Jolla

map
next page

Summary of hike: This hike begins on the southern side of La Jolla along the coastal bluffs at Windansea Beach, just south of Marine Street Beach. Windansea Beach is a popular surfing and sunbathing beach backed by smooth rock shelves that extend like fingers from the palisades to the sand, interspersed with tidepools and small pocket coves. The trail follows the coastline 0.8 miles through La Jolla Strand Park and Hermosa Terrace Park, a small sandy beach tucked between slabs of slick rock formations.

Driving directions: NORTHBOUND: From I-5 (San Diego Freeway) near La Jolla, take the Ardath Road exit, and head 2.5 miles west to Prospect Place. (Ardath Road merges onto Torrey Pines Road en route.) Turn right on Prospect Place, and drive 1 mile, curving through downtown La Jolla, to La Jolla Boulevard. Curve left and continue 0.6 miles to Westbourne Street. Turn right and go 0.2 miles to Neptune Place at the end of the block on the oceanfront. Park along Neptune Place or on the side streets.

SOUTHBOUND: From I-5 (San Diego Freeway) near La Jolla, take the La Jolla Village Drive exit, and head 1.6 miles west to Torrey Pines Road. Turn left and drive 2.7 miles to Prospect Place. Turn right on Prospect Place, and follow the directions above.

Hiking directions: Take the blufftop path south, parallel to Neptune Place, 20 feet above the ocean. On the ledge below, an enormous rock slab juts out to sea. From Westbourne Street to Rosemont Street, five stairways lead from the bluffs to the rock terrace with tidepools. At the west end of Bonair Street, a cabana with a palm-leaf roof sits on the rock slab overlooking the ocean. In less than a half mile, the path ends at Hermosa Terrace Park by Palomar Avenue. Descend to the flat rock between La Jolla Strand Park and Hermosa Terrace Park. Continue south, rounding the point to a beach access at 6204 Camino de la Costa (60 yards northwest of Avenida Cortez). Return by retracing your steps or by looping back on Camino de la Costa.

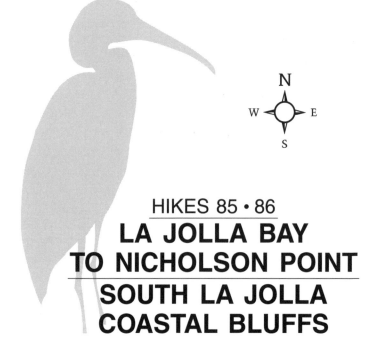

N
W ← → E
S

HIKES 85 • 86
LA JOLLA BAY
TO NICHOLSON POINT
SOUTH LA JOLLA
COASTAL BLUFFS

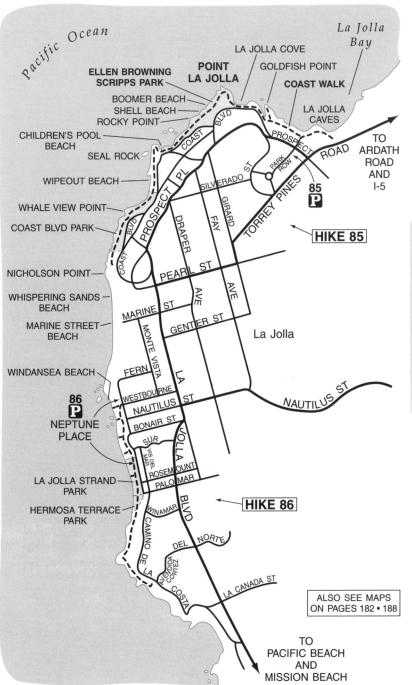

Pacific Ocean

La Jolla Bay

LA JOLLA COVE

POINT
LA JOLLA

GOLDFISH POINT

ELLEN BROWNING
SCRIPPS PARK

COAST WALK

BOOMER BEACH
SHELL BEACH
ROCKY POINT

LA JOLLA
CAVES

CHILDREN'S POOL
BEACH

PROSPECT

SEAL ROCK

ROAD

TO
ARDATH
ROAD
AND
I-5

WIPEOUT BEACH

COAST

BLVD

PARK ROW

SILVERADO ST

WHALE VIEW POINT

PROSPECT PL.

GIRARD

SILVERADO ST

FAY

TORREY PINES

85
P

HIKE 85

COAST BLVD PARK

DRAPER

COAST BLVD

NICHOLSON POINT

PEARL ST

AVE

AVE

WHISPERING SANDS
BEACH

MARINE ST

ST

GENTER ST

La Jolla

MARINE STREET
BEACH

MONTE VISTA

LA

SAN

WINDANSEA BEACH

FERN

JOLLA

ST

NAUTILUS ST

86
P
NEPTUNE
PLACE

WESTBOURNE

NAUTILUS

ST

BONAIR ST

DIEGO

SUR

VIS DEL MAR

JOLLA

COUNTY

LA JOLLA STRAND
PARK

ROSEMOUNT

PALOMAR

BLVD

HERMOSA TERRACE
PARK

WINAMAR

HIKE 86

CAMINO DE LA

DEL NORTE

AVENIDA CORTEZ

COSTA

LA CANADA ST

ALSO SEE MAPS
ON PAGES 182 • 188

TO
PACIFIC BEACH
AND
MISSION BEACH

Hike 87
Tourmaline Surfing Park
to Pacific Beach Park

Hiking distance: 2 miles round trip
Hiking time: 1 hour
Elevation gain: 50 feet
Maps: U.S.G.S. La Jolla

Summary of hike: Tourmaline Surfing Park is a rocky beach on the border of La Jolla and Pacific Beach, just south of False Point. It is a popular surfing, windsurfing, fishing, kayaking, and diving beach. (Swimming is not allowed.) The beach stretches one mile to Crystal Pier, a 720-foot public fishing pier at the foot of Garnet Avenue, the main street through Pacific Beach. Originally built in 1926, Crystal Pier has a row of rental cottages. It is the only pier on the west coast that provides over-the-ocean lodging. This coastline hike also passes through Palisades Park and Pacific Beach Park. Palisades Park is a grassy bluff-top park with paths that lead from the 50-foot bluffs to the wide, sandy beach. Pacific Beach Park is a landscaped park with benches on the low, sloping bluffs near Crystal Pier in the heart of Pacific Beach. For further hiking, parallel pedestrian and bicycle paths line Pacific Beach, connecting it to Mission Beach Park (Hike 89).

Driving directions: NORTHBOUND: From I-5 (San Diego Freeway) in Pacific Beach, take the Grand Avenue exit, and curve west 2.8 miles to Mission Boulevard. Turn right and drive 0.9 miles to Tourmaline Street. Turn left and go a couple of blocks to the oceanfront parking lot at the end of the street.

SOUTHBOUND: From I-5 (San Diego Freeway) in Pacific Beach, take the Garnet Avenue exit. Turn right on Garnet Avenue, and head 1.1 miles west to Lamont Street, where Garnet Avenue merges with Grand Avenue. (Garnet Avenue becomes Balboa Avenue en route.) Continue on Grand Avenue 1.2 miles west to Mission Boulevard. Turn right and follow the directions above.

Hiking directions: Walk to the oceanfront at Tourmaline Surfing Park, and follow the hard-packed sand south (left) beneath the 50-foot cliffs. In a couple hundred yards, head up the staircase that leads up the bluffs to Loring Street or a second staircase 120 yards south. Both stairs lead to a path atop the bluffs. Follow the grassy blufftop through Palisades Park for three blocks, from Loring Street to Law Street, crossing a ravine en route. Pick up the paved walking/biking path, hugging the edge of the cliffs. The palm-lined path passes beachfront homes and resorts. A sloping path leads to sandy Pacific Beach Park by Diamond Street. Stroll along the boardwalk to Crystal Pier at the west end of Garnet Avenue. The east half of this unique pier is lined with vacation homes. The boardwalk passes shops and eateries for a quarter mile to Thomas Avenue, where the walk narrows. This is our turnaround spot.

To hike further, continue south on the narrow promenade into Mission Beach. The walkway ends at Mission Point along the Mission Bay Harbor Channel (Hike 89).

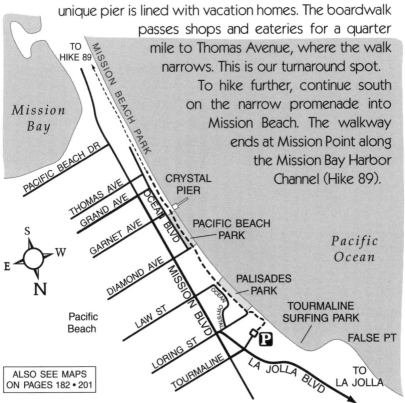

ALSO SEE MAPS
ON PAGES 182 • 201

TOURMALINE SURFING PARK
PACIFIC BEACH

Mission Bay Park
HIKES 88—90

Mission Bay Park was once an enormous marsh formed by the delta of the San Diego River, originally named False Bay by Juan Rodriguez Cabrillo in 1542. The parkland encompasses more than 4,600 acres, located just north of the city of San Diego and south of Pacific Beach.

In the early 1960s, the wetland was transformed into a recreational paradise by dredging, filling, and landscaping. Mission Bay is now the largest facility of its kind in the world, with 11 marinas, 27 miles of shoreline, 17 miles of sandy beaches, and more than 20 miles of waterfront walking and running paths. The diverse park includes islands, coves, inlets, grassy parks, beaches, water-sport centers, and Sea World, a 150-acre marine park opened in 1964. The aquatic playground is a popular spot for swimming, snorkeling, boating, kayaking, windsurfing, water skiing, picnicking and camping.

Mission Beach Park is on the narrow peninsula between the ocean and Mission Bay, directly west of Mission Bay Park. It has a wide, sandy beach that stretches two miles, from just south of Pacific Beach Drive to the Mission Bay Channel. A boardwalk extends along the beach. The walkway connects Mission Beach with Pacific Beach, from the channel to Palisades Park (Hike 87).

Hikes 88, 89, and 90 explore the east, west, and north sides of Mission Bay on paved, shoreline paths.

Hike 88
Crown Point Shores to Riviera Shores
MISSION BAY PARK: NORTH SHORE

Hiking distance: 2.6 miles round trip
Hiking time: 1.5 hours
Elevation gain: 30 feet
Maps: U.S.G.S. La Jolla

map
page 201

Summary of hike: This hike begins next to Fiesta Bay at Crown Point Shores on the south edge of the Kendall-Frost

Marsh Reserve. The reserve is a 16-acre salt marsh that is adjacent to the mudflats and open waters of the 88-acre Northern Wildlife Preserve. This area has the only remaining natural vegetation that survived the wetland community's transformation into the Mission Bay recreational playground. It is an ecological study area and remains a protected feeding and nesting area for migratory and resident birds. A paved path begins at the grassland park, with a sandy beach and picnic areas. The path follows the perimeter of the Crown Point Peninsula, from Fiesta Bay to Riviera Shores, a bluff-backed sandy beach in Sail Bay.

Driving directions: NORTHBOUND: From I-5 (San Diego Freeway) in Pacific Beach, take the Grand Avenue exit, and curve west 1.6 miles to Lamont Street. Turn left and continue 0.6 miles south to Crown Point Drive. Curve right 0.3 miles to the parking lot on the left. Turn left into the parking lot, and curve left to the far north end.

SOUTHBOUND: From I-5 (San Diego Freeway) in Pacific Beach, take the Garnet Avenue exit. Turn right on Garnet Avenue, and head 1.1 miles west to Lamont Street. (Garnet Avenue becomes Balboa Avenue en route.) Turn left and continue 0.6 miles south to Crown Point Drive, following the directions above.

Hiking directions: Start from the north end of the parking lot, at the south edge of the fenced Kendall-Frost Marsh Reserve. Take the paved path and head south through the grassy parkland, overlooking Fiesta Bay, the Ski Islands, UCSD, and downtown San Diego. At a half mile, leave the grassy park and follow the back end of a wide, sandy beach. Cross under the Ingraham Street Bridge along Fisherman's Channel, leaving Fiesta Bay and entering Sail Bay. Views open up to the Mission Beach area across the bay. Follow the edge of the bay beneath the 35-foot cliffs. Along the way, staircases climb the hillside to the bluffs on Riviera Drive. At 1.3 miles, a paved ramp climbs to Riviera Drive near the upper end of Sail Bay. This is a good turnaround spot.

To continue hiking, the path curves around the west side of

Sail Bay in front of apartments, condos, and hotels to Mission Beach.

Hike 89
Mission Point to Mission Bay Park
MISSION BAY PARK · MISSION BEACH

Hiking distance: 2.8 miles round trip
Hiking time: 1.5 hours
Elevation gain: Level
Maps: U.S.G.S. La Jolla

map
next page

Summary of hike: This hike is a loop that begins on the west edge of Mission Bay and returns along the oceanfront board-walk. The hike follows Bay Walk, a paved path on the banks of Mariners Basin. The path connects Mission Point at the channel to Mission Bay Park at Bonita Cove (a swimming area). The hike returns along Ocean Front Walk, a popular walking, jogging, roller-skating, skateboarding, biking and people-watching promenade. The Ocean Front Walk passes Belmont Park, an old amusement park with a renovated 1925 roller coaster and The Plunge, a vast 175-foot-long swimming pool. The beach ends at Point Medanos by the jetty at the mouth of the Mission Bay Channel.

Driving directions: From I-5 (San Diego Freeway) near Ocean Beach, take I-8 (Ocean Beach Freeway) 2 miles west to the West Mission Bay Drive exit. Turn right and drive 2.2 miles, crossing over the San Diego River and Mission Bay Channel, to Mission Boulevard. Turn left and continue 1 mile south to the far end of the parking lot at Mission Point.

NORTHBOUND: From I-5 (San Diego Freeway) in Pacific Beach, take the Grand Avenue exit, and curve west 2.8 miles to Mission Boulevard. Turn left and continue 1 mile south to the far end of the parking lot at Mission Point.

SOUTHBOUND: From I-5 (San Diego Freeway) in Pacific Beach, take the Garnet Avenue exit. Turn right on Garnet Avenue, and head 1.1 miles west to Lamont Street, where Garnet Avenue merges with Grand Avenue. (Garnet Avenue becomes Balboa Avenue en route.) Continue on Grand Avenue 1.2 miles west to Mission Boulevard. Turn left and continue 1 mile south to the far end of the parking lot at Mission Point.

Hiking directions: From Mission Point on the northeast edge of the Mission Bay Channel, the path circles the park around the point. Follow the bay and curve north along the sandy waterfront, between homes on the left and Mariners Basin on the right. At 0.9 miles, near the north end of Mariners Basin, the pathway open up into Mission Bay Park and a grassy knoll. The park and path wrap around Bonita Cove to Mariners Point on the southeast tip of the cove, across the basin from the trailhead. Return to Mission Boulevard, and cross the street to Belmont Park on the oceanfront. Stroll south on the oceanfront boardwalk to a large grassy park at the mouth of the Mission Bay Channel. Across the channel is Dog Beach at Ocean Beach Park (Hike 92). Dogs can be seen frolicking on the sand and in the water. Follow the bay channel inland, returning to the trailhead at Mission Point.

Hike 90
De Anza Cove to Tecolote Creek
MISSION BAY PARK: EAST SHORE

Hiking distance: 4.6 miles round trip
Hiking time: 2.5 hours
Elevation gain: Level
Maps: U.S.G.S. La Jolla

map
next page

Summary of hike: This hike follows the east shore of Mission Bay from De Anza Cove to Tecolote Creek. The creek flows from Tecolote Canyon into the Pacific Passageway, a waterway between the bay's east shore and Fiesta Island. A marshy wetland is formed at the mouth of the creek as it enters the bay. The east shore is lined with landscaped parklands, picnic areas, sandy beaches, and is home to the Mission Bay Visitor Center. The hike starts at De Anza Cove, a charming little bay

SAN DIEGO COUNTY

100 Great Hikes - **199**

with a boat dock, sandy beach, and picnic spots. A paved path follows the eastern shoreline, overlooking barren Fiesta Island. En route, the trail passes a series of beaches and strolls through Playa Pacifica and Tecolote Shores, two grassland parks.

Driving directions: From I-5 (San Diego Freeway) in Mission Bay, take the Clairmont Drive exit. Head west one block to Mission Bay Drive by the visitor center. Turn right and drive 0.9 miles to De Anza Road. Turn left and quickly turn left again into the De Anza Cove parking lot.

Hiking directions: Take the paved path from the west end of De Anza Cove and head east. Walk through the grassy park along the north shore of the cove. Beyond the cove, curve right and follow the eastern shoreline, parallel to I-5. At 0.6 miles, pass a sandy beach and boat launch. Stroll past a group of palm trees where boulders line the bay, reaching the Mission Bay Visitor Center at 0.9 miles. Continue through Playa Pacifica, a sandy beach backed by rolling grasslands and palm trees, with views across the Pacific Passage to desolate Fiesta Island. The paved path meanders through the park, fronting a sandy beach. Make a sweeping S-curve, and cross a park road to the bay side of the Hilton Hotel at 1.6 miles. Follow the shoreline between the hotel and the sandy beach, passing a carved relief mural and mature pine trees. Beyond the hotel, the palm-lined trail winds through Tecolote Shores, an expansive grassland with a playground area. Curve around the playground towards the bridge over Tecolote Creek. Take the unpaved path along the shoreline lagoon, merging with the paved path at the bridge at 2.3 miles. This is the turnaround spot.

N
W ◆ E
S

HIKES 88–90
MISSION BAY

TO
LA JOLLA

KATE SESSIONS
PARK

TURQUOISE

LA JOLLA

87
CRYSTAL
PIER

MISSION BLVD

Pacific Ocean

MISSION BEACH PARK

SOLEDAD MTN RD

LAMONT ST

GARNET AVE

BALBOA AVE

GARNET AVE

GRAND AVE

BALBOA AVE

PACIFIC BEACH DR

INGRAHAM

RIVIERA DR

CROWN POINT DR

RIVIERA SHORES

CROWN POINT SHORES

Sail
Bay

Mission

MISSION BAY PARK

BELMONT
PARK

Bonita
Cove

Mariners Basin

W. MISSION BAY DR

MARINERS
POINT

MISSION PT

POINT
MEDANOS

89
P

Mission Bay Channel

JETTY

DOG BEACH

92

OCEAN
BEACH
PIER

93

BACON ST

SUNSET CLIFFS

VOLTAIRE ST

NIAGARA AVE

MISSION BAY DR

5

90
P

De Anza Cove

NORTHERN
WILDLIFE
PRESERVE

VISITOR
CENTER

CLAIREMONT

Fiesta
Bay

88
P

SKI
ISLANDS

PLAYA
PACIFICA

HILTON

MISSION BAY

MORENA BLVD

Fisherman's
Channel

Bay

Fiesta
Island

FIESTA
ISLAND

TECOLOTE
SHORES

Tecolote
Creek

TO
TECOLOTE
CANYON
(HIKE 91)

Pacific Passageway

SEA
WORLD

SEA WORLD DR

San Diego River

OCEAN BEACH BLVD

WEST POINT LOMA BLVD

SPORTS ARENA BLVD

FWY

8

TO
SAN DIEGO

NIMITZ BLVD

CHATSWORTH BLVD

ROSECRANS ST

5

SAN DIEGO COUNTY

ALSO SEE MAPS ON
PAGES 182 • 195 • 207

Hike 91
Tecolote Canyon Natural Park

Hiking distance: 5.5 miles round trip
Hiking time: 3 hours
Elevation gain: 250 feet
Maps: U.S.G.S. La Jolla

Summary of hike: Tecolote Canyon Natural Park is a peaceful 900-acre refuge surrounded by urban development in the communities of Clairmont, Bay Park, and Linda Vista. The natural park, just north of San Diego, is named for the owl that makes its home in the canyon. Seasonal Tecolote Creek meanders for miles through the canyon on its journey to the east shore of Mission Bay, less than a mile away. Large groves of live oak, willow, and sycamore trees line the canyon floor, with chaparral and coastal sage scrub covering the hillsides. The park is home to a wide variety of wildlife, including coyote, fox, bobcat, roadrunners, hawks, quail, and doves. The dog-friendly park has 6.5 miles of trails that connect from 9 trailheads. This hike begins at the main (south) entrance by the nature center at the mouth of the canyon. The hike explores the southern section of the park through open meadows and lush riparian thickets.

Driving directions: From I-5 (San Diego Freeway) by Mission Bay, take the Sea World Drive/Tecolote Canyon exit, and head 0.5 miles east to Tecolote Canyon Natural Park. Drive straight ahead 0.1 miles to the parking lot at the end of the road by the nature center.

Hiking directions: After visiting the nature center, take the wide dirt path into Tecolote Canyon along the south side of the creek. The University of San Diego Catholic Church, with its large dome roof and steeple, sits prominently atop the south canyon bluff. Continue up the canyon to a trail split at just under a mile. The right fork leaves the park to Via Las Cumbres. Stay to the left on the main trail, crossing under the power lines. Pass a row of towering eucalyptus trees and a few random sycamores. At

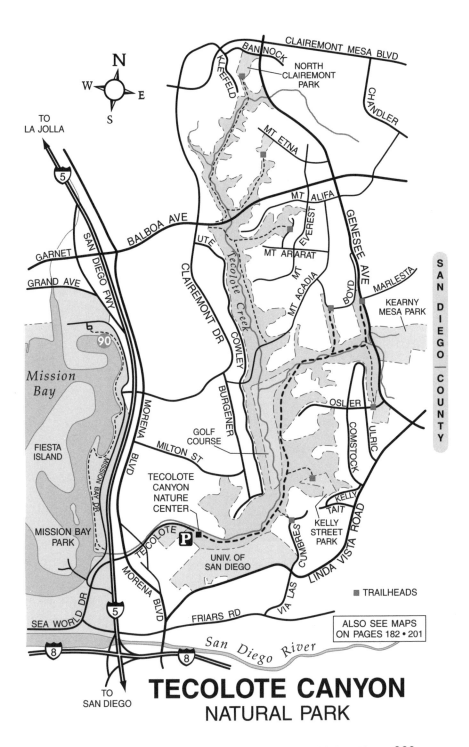

N
W E
S

TO
LA JOLLA

CLAIREMONT MESA BLVD

BAN NOCK

KLEEFELD

NORTH
CLAIREMONT
PARK

CHANDLER

MT ETNA

MT ALIFA

BALBOA AVE

UTE

Tecolote Creek

GENESEE AVE

EVEREST

MARLESTA

GARNET

SAN DIEGO FWY

CLAIREMONT DR

COWLEY

MT ARARAT

MT ACADIA

BOYD

KEARNY
MESA PARK

**S
A
N

D
I
E
G
O

C
O
U
N
T
Y**

GRAND AVE

*Mission
Bay*

90

BURGENER

OSLER

ULRIC

COMSTOCK

MORENA BLVD

GOLF
COURSE

MILTON ST

KELLY

TAIT

FIESTA
ISLAND

MISSION BAY DR

TECOLOTE
CANYON
NATURE
CENTER

KELLY
STREET
PARK

LINDA VISTA ROAD

MISSION BAY
PARK

TECOLOTE

P

UNIV. OF
SAN DIEGO

CUMBRES

■ TRAILHEADS

MORENA BLVD

5

VIA LAS

ALSO SEE MAPS
ON PAGES 182 • 201

SEA WORLD DR

FRIARS RD

8

San Diego River

8

TO
SAN DIEGO

TECOLOTE CANYON
NATURAL PARK

1.2 miles, the trail reaches the Tecolote Canyon Golf Course via a few connecting paths. Follow the trail bordering the golf course. Ascend the hill, climbing high above the golf course, and cross the rolling terrain. After a series of short, steep dips and rises, the path levels out and traverses the hillside. Leave the golf course behind, and enter the most picturesque portion of the hike. Follow the watercourse upstream on a grassy flat through shaded oak glens with scattered sycamores and palms. As the canyon narrows and the foliage thickens, the path crosses the stream several times. After the third crossing, the unsigned Boyd Trail bears left and climbs the west wall of a side canyon to Boyd Avenue in a residential area. Return into Tecolote Canyon and cross a concrete spillway. Gradually ascend the north canyon wall, then drop back down to the streambed. Follow the streambed 30 yards and curve left, emerging on Genesee Avenue 0.2 miles south of Marlesta Drive. Return by retracing your route.

Hike 92
Ocean Beach Park
Dog Beach to Ocean Beach Pier

Hiking distance: 2 miles round trip
Hiking time: 1 hour
Elevation gain: Level
Maps: U.S.G.S. La Jolla and Point Loma

map
next page

Summary of hike: Dog Beach is located on the north end of Ocean Beach along the mouth of the San Diego River and across the harbor channel from Mission Bay. It is a favorite oceanfront spot among canines. Nearly every car arrival has an enthusiastic, tail-wagging dog, and every departure has a tired and satisfied pooch. It is the only city beach in San Diego that allows dogs to run free (and one of three in the county, along with Del Mar and Coronado). To the east are sand dunes, marshland, and inter-tidal communities. The dunes act as a barrier for the calm estuary, which receives fresh water from the river and salt water from the ocean. To the south is the Ocean Beach Pier, a concrete, 2,100-foot T-shaped fishing pier. The sandy beach between Dog Beach and the pier is a popular surfing and swimming area with a paved promenade and grassy picnic grounds. This hike begins at Dog Beach and explores the wetlands to the east and the promenade south to the pier.

Driving directions: From I-5 (San Diego Freeway) in San Diego, exit on the Ocean Beach Freeway (Highway 8), and head 2 miles west to the end of the freeway. Turn left on Sunset Cliffs Boulevard, and continue 0.5 miles to West Point Loma Boulevard. Turn right and drive 0.5 miles to Voltaire Street. Park in the oceanfront parking lot on the right.

Hiking directions: Walk out to sandy Dog Beach at the north tip of Ocean Beach Park. From the parking lot to the Mission Bay Channel, dogs are running, swimming, digging, sniffing, and playing. Two paths head east along the San Diego River. A paved path follows the back end of Dog Beach, parallel to the south edge of the wetland estuary and the river. The path leads into Robb Field, a grassy park with ball fields and paved walkways. At the north end of sandy Dog Beach, by the Mission Bay Channel, a path crosses the dunes between the channel and the north edge of the estuary. Follow the sandspit onto the San Diego River floodway path. Return to the ocean by the rocky south jetty, separating Dog Beach from the rest of Ocean Beach. Stroll south on the wide, sandy beach. Near the lifeguard station, a grassy park backs the beach. A paved promenade leads to the Ocean Beach Pier and access stairs. On the south side of the pier are flat, water-carved rock formations with tidepools. The boardwalk ends where steps drop down to the rock shelf. This is our turnaround area.

To continue walking, follow the directions to Pescadero Beach (Hike 93).

Hike 93
Ocean Beach Pier to Pescadero Beach

Hiking distance: 1.5 miles round trip
Hiking time: 1 hour
Elevation gain: 20 feet
Maps: U.S.G.S. Point Loma

Summary of hike: Ocean Beach extends from the San Diego River floodway to the bluff-backed beach off of Pescadero Avenue. Ocean Beach Pier lies inbetween, a T-shaped fishing pier at the foot of Niagara Avenue. It is the longest pier on the west coast, extending 2,100 feet over the water. The shoreline between the pier and Pescadero Beach has a water-carved rock shelf extending out to sea, with small pocket beaches, rocky crevices, and tidepools. The beach is backed by 30-foot bluffs with five sets of stairways that descend to the rocky beach. The whole day can easily be spent exploring the various rock ledges and tidepools. This low-tide hike begins at the pier and follows the flat rock ledges and seawalls to the stairway beneath Pescadero Avenue.

Driving directions: From I-5 (San Diego Freeway) in San Diego, exit on the Ocean Beach Freeway (Highway 8), and head 2 miles west to the end of the freeway. Turn left on Sunset Cliffs Boulevard, and continue 0.5 miles to West Point Loma Boulevard. Turn right and drive 0.5 miles to Voltaire Street. Turn into the oceanfront parking lot on the right. Curve left and drive 0.4 miles to the south end of the parking lot near the Ocean Beach Pier.

Hiking directions: Take the paved boardwalk to the Ocean Beach Pier. Detour up the stairs and out on the pier to view the anglers' "catch of the day" and feel the ocean breezes. Return and continue south 100 yards to the end of the boardwalk at the water-carved rock formations with tidepools. During low tide, when it is safe, walk down the steps to the rock shelf. Stroll south along the shelf, passing tiny, sandy beach pockets.

A staircase leads up the cliffs to Santa Cruz Avenue by a gorgeous pocket beach bordered by rock fingers jutting out to sea. Scramble across the hillside path, and pick up the raised, paved path, winding along the edge of the cliffs. Pass an offshore formation known as Alligator Rock. The paved path ends by a stairway leading up the cliffs to Orchard Avenue by Cable Street. At the south end of Cable Street, a paved cliffside path traverses the cliffs again to another pocket beach and stairway at Pescadero Drive. To return, retrace your steps or take Cable Street and zigzag back to the Ocean Beach Pier.

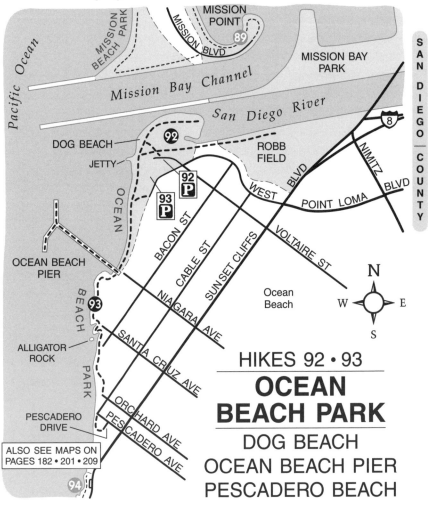

HIKES 92 • 93

OCEAN BEACH PARK

DOG BEACH
OCEAN BEACH PIER
PESCADERO BEACH

Hike 94
Sunset Cliffs Park

Hiking distance: 3.6 miles round trip
Hiking time: 2 hours
Elevation gain: 100 feet
Maps: U.S.G.S. Point Loma

Summary of hike: Sunset Cliffs Park sits on the west edge of Point Loma, a 4-mile long peninsula that looks like a bent index finger. Stretching south from Ocean Beach, the dramatic 400-foot high promontory separates the ocean from San Diego Bay. Steep 50-foot vertical cliffs line the long and narrow ocean-front park that overlooks a scalloped coastline with offshore rocks, sea arches, sea caves, reefs, kelp beds, hidden sandy coves, and rocky beaches (back cover photo). An exposed plateau of flat rocks with tidepools extends out to sea. Clifftop trails skirt the jagged, unstable edge of the bluffs, and eroding paths lead down the striated cliffs to pocket beaches. At the west end of Ladera Street, a stairway leads to the rocky shoreline. South of Ladera Street, informal trails wind through the wide, sloping terrace surrounded by eucalyptus groves beneath Point Loma Nazarine University.

Driving directions: From I-5 (San Diego Freeway) in San Diego, exit on the Ocean Beach Freeway (Highway 8), and head 2 miles west to the end of the freeway. Turn left on Sunset Cliffs Boulevard, and drive 1.9 miles to the Sunset Cliffs ocean-front parking lot on the right.

Hiking directions: Follow the bluff path south atop the multi-level, eroding sedimentary formations, parallel to Sunset Cliffs Boulevard. Sloping rock fingers jut out to sea, with caves, crevices, arches, and small sandy coves. There are endless opportunities to walk out on the fingers of land, explore tide-pools, and marvel at the landscape. Pass Osprey Point to the gorgeous, bird-covered offshore rocks at Pappy's Point. The bluffs have eroded back to Sunset Cliffs Boulevard by Ross

Rock, adjacent to Froude Street. At 0.8 miles, pass Luscomb's Point, a wide flat with beaches, sheer vertical cliffs, caves, and arches. At 1.2 miles, Sunset Cliffs Boulevard ends at Ladera Street. Paths wind along the bluffs as Ladera Street veers inland. A stairway leads down to a cove and a sandy beach by wave-cut reefs. Continue along the bluffs, curving inland through eucalyptus groves. Skirt around a home and a dirt parking lot off of Ladera Street and Cornish Drive. Trails meander through the expansive south section of Sunset Cliffs Park. Cross the wide, sloping park on the eroding, multi-level bluffs through pine and eucalyptus groves. Surfer paths descend over 100 feet to the beach. The trails end at a military base fence above Newbreak Beach and below Point Loma Nazarine University. Return by retracing your steps.

ALSO SEE MAPS
ON PAGES 182 • 207

SUNSET CLIFFS PARK

Point Loma • Cabrillo National Monument
HIKES 95—96

Point Loma stretches south from Ocean Beach along a 4-mile long finger of land that separates San Diego Bay from the ocean. Perched at the southern end of this sandstone peninsula is Cabrillo National Monument, a dramatic 144-acre park. From the headland are epic views of the coastline south to Mexico, including San Diego Bay, Shelter Island, Harbor Island, Coronado, the Embarcadero, the San Diego skyline, Tijuana, and the Coronado Islands off the coast of Mexico. The national monument commemorates Portuguese explorer Juan Rodriguez Cabrillo, the first European to set foot on the shores of the west coast when he sailed into San Diego Bay in 1542, only 50 years after Columbus landed in America. Within the park is an interpretive center with exhibits, a museum, a gift shop, and a whale-watching overlook. On the 422-foot summit is a restored New England-style lighthouse, dating back to 1854. From December through March, it is a great spot for viewing the annual migration of the gray whale from their arctic summer feeding grounds to their breeding grounds in the bays of Baja California.

Hike 95
Bayside Trail
CABRILLO NATIONAL MONUMENT

Hiking distance: 3 miles round trip
Hiking time: 1.5 hours
Elevation gain: 300 feet
Maps: U.S.G.S. Point Loma

map next page

Summary of hike: The Bayside Trail descends 300 feet down the cliffs on the east (bayside) slope of Point Loma. The 1.5-mile trail, an old U.S. Army roadway, winds down the hillside through chaparral and native sage scrub from high above San Diego Bay. From the cliffside perch are breathtaking vistas of the bay, including small sailboats, fishing boats, gigantic U.S.

Navy ships, ocean liners maneuvering in and out of the harbor, as well as passenger planes and Navy jets flying in and out of the airports. The interpretive trail has panels about the area's natural and cultural history. En route, the trail passes remnants of an abandoned military defense system with bunkers that protected the harbor in both World Wars. The hike begins near the 422-foot crest of the promontory by the historic lighthouse.

Driving directions: Cabrillo National Monument is located at the end of Catalina Boulevard on the southern tip of Point Loma.

SOUTHBOUND: From I-5 (San Diego Freeway) in San Diego, take the Rosecrans Street (209) exit, and head 3 miles southwest to Canon Street. Turn right and drive 1.3 miles to Catalina Boulevard. Turn left and continue 3.1 miles to a road split. (Catalina Boulevard becomes Cabrillo Memorial Drive en route.) Stay to the left and enter Cabrillo National Monument. Continue a quarter mile to the end of the road at the visitor center parking lot. An entrance fee is required.

NORTHBOUND: From I-5 (San Diego Freeway) in San Diego, take the Pacific Highway exit. Drive 1.6 miles and curve left onto Barnett Avenue. Continue another mile to Rosecrans Street (209). Turn left and continue 2 miles to Canon Street. Turn right and follow the directions above.

Hiking directions: Walk south, up the paved sidewalk from the visitor center, to the Old Point Loma Lighthouse on the right. Paved and natural paths loop around the bluffs, overlooking both the Pacific Ocean and San Diego Bay. After visiting the lighthouse, take the road to the left. Head down the hillside to a signed path on the left with a sitting bench. Bear left on the graveled Bayside Trail, winding through coastal sage scrub, cactus, and yucca. Weave in and out of small canyons on a gradual descent. Pass eroded sandstone formations with caves; old military bunkers; and interpretive panels about the vegetation, wildlife, water, and birds. The trail ends 300 feet below the visitor center at the fenced naval base boundary. Return along the same route.

Hike 96
Point Loma Tidepools and Bluff Trail
CABRILLO NATIONAL MONUMENT

Hiking distance: 1.2 miles round trip
Hiking time: 45 minutes
Elevation gain: 30 feet
Maps: U.S.G.S. Point Loma

Summary of hike: This hike explores the Point Loma tide-pools along the western (ocean) shore of the promontory. The area is home to some of the finest tidepools in southern California. From below the 400-foot sandstone cliffs, the trail strolls along the rugged, rocky bluffs and shoreline through the intertidal zone, passing rock outcrops, offshore reefs, pounding surf, and tidepools. A self-guiding trail with exhibits explains the plants, animals, and history of the area. Although the area is magnificent to explore at any time, low tide is the best time to view the tidepools.

Driving directions: Cabrillo National Monument is located at the end of Catalina Boulevard on the southern tip of Point Loma.

SOUTHBOUND: From I-5 (San Diego Freeway) in San Diego, take the Rosecrans Street (209) exit, and head 3 miles southwest to Canon Street. Turn right and drive 1.3 miles to Catalina Boulevard. Turn left and continue 3.1 miles to a road split. (Catalina Boulevard becomes Cabrillo Memorial Drive en route.) Bear right on Cabrillo Road, and descend 0.8 miles to the parking lot on the left at the oceanfront bluffs.

NORTHBOUND: From I-5 (San Diego Freeway) in San Diego, take the Pacific Highway exit. Drive 1.6 miles and curve left onto Barnett Avenue. Continue another mile to Rosecrans Street (209). Turn left and continue 2 miles to Canon Street. Turn right and follow the directions above.

Hiking directions: Take the signed path north past the information board. The upper route follows the bluffs and meanders along the scalloped coastline on flat, terraced rock shelves. The tidepools are accessed from the lower route and can be safely explored at low tide. Choose your own path. Trails descend from the surf-carved cliffs to the rocky beach, with intriguing inlets, coves, and tide-pools. The upper path traverses above the shoreline on the rock ledges overlooking the ocean. The bluff path ends at a parking area on the far north end of the road.

TO
OCEAN BEACH
AND
SAN DIEGO

(CATALINA BLVD.)
CABRILLO

FORT ROSECRANS
MILITARY
RESERVATION

MEMORIAL DR

CABRILLO RD

P

P

95
P

VISITOR
CENTER

STATUE

OLD POINT LOMA
LIGHTHOUSE

*Pacific
Ocean*

WHALE
OVERLOOK

96
P

N

W ⊕ E

S

POINT LOMA
LIGHT STATION

ALSO SEE MAP
ON PAGE 182

HIKES 95 • 96
POINT LOMA
CABRILLO NATIONAL MONUMENT

Hike 97
Centennial Park to Tidelands Park
CORONADO PENINSULA

Hiking distance: 2 miles round trip
Hiking time: 1 hour
Elevation gain: Level
Maps: U.S.G.S. Point Loma

map next page

Summary of hike: The Coronado Peninsula lies in the heart of San Diego Bay between the bay and the ocean. This hike follows the picturesque bay from Centennial Park to Tidelands Park, with sweeping views of downtown San Diego. The Coronado Peninsula is thought of (and referred to) as an island. It is actually attached to the mainland by Silver Strand, a quarter-mile-wide sand spit running 7 miles from North Island to Imperial Beach. The other land access to the "almost-an-island" peninsula is the arched 2.3-mile Coronado Toll Bridge, connecting Coronado to the city of San Diego. Centennial Park and Tidelands Park sit on the bay side of Coronado, connected by a shoreline promenade. Centennial Park is a grassy park with a small sandy beach and a rose garden. Adjacent to the park is Old Ferry Landing, the location for catching the ferry to San Diego, and Ferry Landing Marketplace. The market is lined with galleries, boutiques, and restaurants. Tidelands Park is a 22-acre tree-shaded grassland park on the northeast corner of Coronado. The bayfront park has a sandy beach, picnic tables, and a walking/biking path that skirts the bay, passing under the towering Coronado Toll Bridge.

Driving directions: From I-5 (San Diego Freeway) south of downtown San Diego, take the Coronado Toll Bridge (Highway 75) exit. Cross San Diego Bay into Coronado to Orange Avenue (Highway 75). Turn right and drive 2 blocks to 1st Street. Parking is available along 1st Street, and a parking lot is on the bay side of 1st Street between A Avenue and B Avenue.

Hiking directions: From 1st Street and Orange Avenue, walk towards San Diego Bay, passing shops into Centennial Park fronting the bay. Walk to the right to the Coronado Ferry Pier and Ferry Landing Marketplace. After strolling out on the pier, continue east towards the prominent Coronado Bridge. As you near the bridge, the path curves right on the bay side of the expansive grasslands of Tidelands Park. A sandy beach lines the bay. At the south end of the park, the walking/biking path continues under Coronado Bridge along the perimeter of the 130-acre Coronado Golf Course. The path ends in a quarter mile at Glorietta Boulevard. Return to Centennial Park, with great views of Point Loma, the bay, and the naval ships at North Island.

Hike 98
Coronado City Beach and
Coronado Shores Beach
CORONADO PENINSULA

Hiking distance: 3.6 miles round trip
Hiking time: 2 hours
Elevation gain: Level
Maps: U.S.G.S. Point Loma

map next page

Summary of hike: Coronado City Beach, on the ocean side of the Coronado Peninsula, is home of the historic Hotel del Coronado, a vast Victorian complex built in 1888. The elegant landmark, dominating the oceanfront landscape, encompasses 33 acres. With 680 rooms, it is one of the largest wooden structures in the world.

The city beach is divided into North, Central, and South Beach, stretching from the magnificent hotel to the North Island Naval Air Station. Within North Beach is a dog-friendly beach known locally as Dog Beach. Adjacent to Dog Beach is Sunset Park, with a large, grassy picnic area.

Coronado Shores Beach runs from South Beach, near the Hotel del Coronado, to Silver Strand State Beach. It is a wide, sandy beach across the boulevard from Glorietta Bay, backed

SAN DIEGO COUNTY

by condominiums and a seawall promenade. The paved path ends at the U.S. Naval Amphibious Base boundary. This hike follows the 1.8-mile beachfront promenade from Coronado Shores Beach, at the naval amphibious base, to North Beach at the naval air station. The coastal views include Point Loma, the Coronado Islands (13 miles offshore), and Tijuana.

Driving directions: From I-5 (San Diego Freeway) south of downtown San Diego, take the Coronado Toll Bridge (Highway 75) exit. Cross San Diego Bay into Coronado to Orange Avenue (Highway 75). Turn left and drive 1.3 miles to Avenida Del Sol. Turn right and park.

Hiking directions: The South Beach Seawall begins at Avenida Del Sol. Head south 0.4 miles, overlooking the ocean with unobstructed views from Point Loma to Tijuana. The paved path ends in less than a half mile at Avenida Lunar by the U.S. Naval Amphibious Base. Return to Avenida Del Sol, and continue north in front of the historic Hotel del Coronado. After exploring the hotel grounds, continue northwest on the public walkway leading through the wide, landscaped corridor of the hotel grounds. Beyond the hotel, the palm-lined sidewalk fronts Central Beach along Ocean Boulevard, reaching the rock wall at North Beach. The walkway ends at the Naval Air Station boundary by Sunset Park and Dog Beach, an off-leash playground for dogs. Return along the same route.

HIKES 97 • 98
CORONADO PENINSULA
CENTENNIAL PARK • TIDELANDS PARK
CORONADO BEACH • CORONADO SHORES

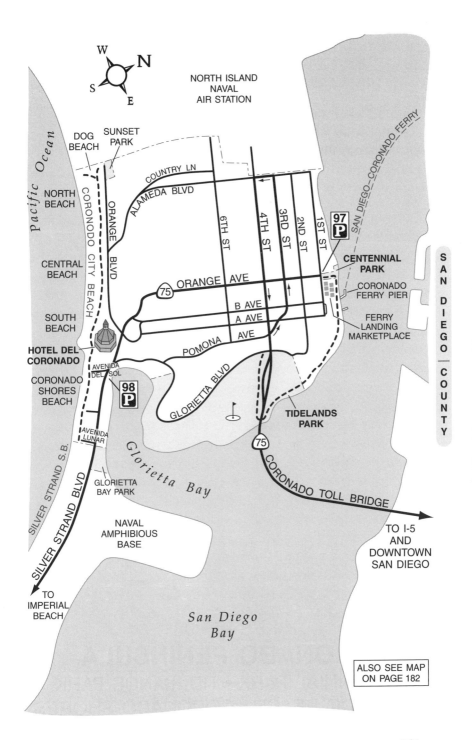

Hike 99
River Mouth—South McCoy Trails
TIJUANA ESTUARY NATIONAL WILDLIFE REFUGE

Hiking distance: 2 miles round trip
Hiking time: 1 hour
Elevation gain: Level
Maps: U.S.G.S. Imperial Beach
       National Estuarine Research Reserve System map

*map
next page*

Summary of hike: The Tijuana River National Estuarine Reserve is located south of San Diego and within view of Mexico. The reserve comprises 2,531 acres of salt marshes, tidal wetlands, mud flats, brackish ponds, vernal pools, riparian habitat, dunes, upland areas, and sandy beaches within the Tijuana River floodplain. The Tijuana River delta is the largest and most diverse wetland in southern California, supporting a wide variety of plants, shorebirds, over 370 species of migratory and resident waterfowl, invertebrates, and fish. Within the reserve is Border Field State Park, located at the United States-Mexico border, and the Tijuana Estuary National Wildlife Refuge in Imperial Beach. Many areas are off limits, but an established 6-mile trail system allows public access while still protecting sensitive estuarine sanctuary. The trails cross the relatively flat terrain, meandering around the open and protected waters. This hike loops through the wildlife refuge, adjacent to the Imperial Beach Naval Auxiliary Landing Field. During the week, a steady stream of helicopters practice take-offs and landings on the adjacent naval air station and can be annoying.

The Tijuana Estuary Visitor Center is located off of Imperial Beach Boulevard and 3rd Street at 301 Caspian Way. (A short trail runs through the slough from the visitor center.)

Driving directions: From I-5 (San Diego Freeway), head 12 miles south of San Diego, and take the Coronado Avenue exit. Turn right and drive 2.2 miles west to 5th Street. (Coronado Avenue becomes Imperial Beach Boulevard en route.) Turn left and go a half mile to the end of 5th Street and park.

The visitor center is located one block off Imperial Beach Boulevard at 3rd Street and Caspian Way.

Hiking directions: Parallel the naval landing strip 30 yards west to the River Mouth Trail. Follow the wide path south on the edge of the Tijuana Estuary National Wildlife Refuge and bordering the Imperial Beach Naval Air Station. At a half mile, curve right and head toward the ocean to a T-junction with the South McCoy Trail. Detour to the left and head 100 yards south to an overlook at trail's end and a bench on the banks of the Tijuana River. Return to the T-junction, and head north on a dry, raised path through the wetlands, passing the return route on the right. Continue north to an overlook at a waterway at the end of the trail. Across the waterway is the end of the trail that begins from the visitor center. Return south to the trail split. Veer left two consecutive times, back to the trailhead.

Hike 100
Imperial Beach—Shoreline Trail
TIJUANA ESTUARY NATIONAL WILDLIFE REFUGE

Hiking distance: 1.2 miles round trip
Hiking time: 40 minutes
Elevation gain: 15 feet
Maps: U.S.G.S. Imperial Beach
      National Estuarine Research Reserve System map

map
next page

Summary of hike: Imperial Beach is a quiet, low-key beach town with a wide, sandy beach strand south of San Diego. The Tijuana River borders the south end of Imperial Beach. To the east is the expansive Tijuana Estuary National Wildlife Refuge (Hike 99). The Tijuana River watershed drains more than 1,700 square miles along the California-Mexico border, with its end point in the estuary. Barrier dunes, formed by sand traveling down river from the mountains, protect the estuary from the ocean forces. Wind and waves have sculpted the sand into dunes, while native vegetation stabilizes the dunes and holds them in place. Without the dunes, there would be no estuary.

S
A
N

D
I
E
G
O

C
O
U
N
T
Y

This hike straddles the dunes between the ocean and the estuary to the mouth of the Tijuana River, where it empties into the Pacific Ocean. Along the way are expansive coastal views extending north to Coronado and Point Loma, south to the hills of Mexico, and 12 miles seaward to the Coronado Islands.

Driving directions: From I-5 (San Diego Freeway) head 12 miles south of San Diego, and take the Coronado Avenue exit. Turn right and drive 2.8 miles west to Seacoast Drive. (Coronado Avenue becomes Imperial Beach Boulevard en route.) Turn left and go 0.7 miles to the trailhead at the end of the road. Parking spaces are on the left.

The Tijuana Estuary Visitor Center is located one block off Imperial Beach Boulevard at 3rd Street and Caspian Way.

Hiking directions: Head south on the boardwalk to an observation platform of the Tijuana Estuary National Wildlife Refuge and an informative panel. Walk toward the rocky beach, and head south up the 15-foot dune. Follow the narrow ridge through a mix of rounded rocks and sand patches, straddling the wide estuary water channel on the left and the ocean on the right. The path descends to the sandy beach and ends at the mouth of the Tijuana River. This is our turnaround spot.

At low tide, it is possible to hike further. Cross the sandbar or small stream, and follow the coastline less than 2 miles to the 10-foot-high fenced border with Mexico at the base of the brown hills and the sprawl of Tijuana across the fence. The river may be too deep to ford at high tide (and too polluted, due to its journey through Tijuana).

HIKES 99 • 100
TIJUANA ESTUARY
RIVER MOUTH • SOUTH McCOY TRAILS
IMPERIAL BEACH–SHORELINE TRAIL

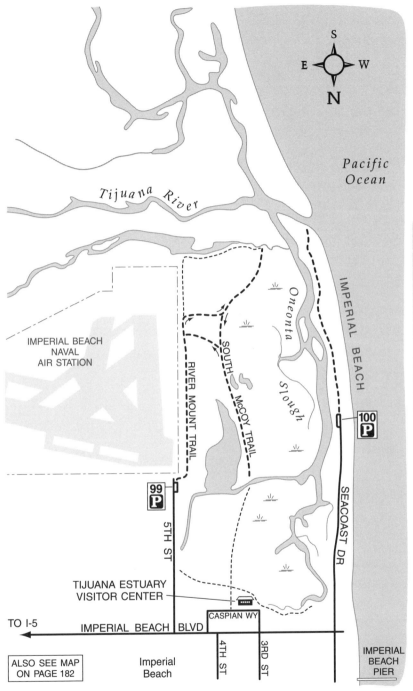

S
E ⊕ W
N

Pacific
Ocean

SAN DIEGO COUNTY

IMPERIAL BEACH NAVAL AIR STATION

Tijuana River

Oneonta Slough

IMPERIAL BEACH

100 P

99 P

RIVER MOUNT TRAIL

SOUTH McCOY TRAIL

SEACOAST DR

5TH ST

TIJUANA ESTUARY VISITOR CENTER

TO I-5

IMPERIAL BEACH BLVD

CASPIAN WY

4TH ST

3RD ST

Imperial Beach

ALSO SEE MAP ON PAGE 182

IMPERIAL BEACH PIER

Other Day Hike Guidebooks

Day Hikes On the California Central Coast 14.95

Day Hikes On the California Southern Coast 14.95

Day Hikes Around Monterey and Carmel 14.95

Day Hikes Around Big Sur 14.95

Day Hikes In San Luis Obispo County, California 14.95

Day Hikes Around Santa Barbara......................... 14.95

Day Hikes Around Ventura County........................ 14.95

Day Hikes Around Los Angeles........................... 14.95

Day Hikes In Yosemite National Park 11.95

Day Hikes In Sequoia and Kings Canyon National Parks 12.95

Day Hikes In Yellowstone National Park 9.95

Day Hikes In Grand Teton National Park 11.95

Day Hikes In the Beartooth Mountains
Red Lodge, Montana to Yellowstone National Park 11.95

Day Hikes Around Bozeman, Montana 11.95

Day Hikes Around Missoula, Montana...................... 11.95

Day Hikes On Oahu..................................... 11.95

Day Hikes On Maui 11.95

Day Hikes On Kauai 11.95

Day Trips On St. Martin 9.95

Day Hikes In Sedona, Arizona............................ 9.95

These books may be purchased at your local bookstore or
outdoor shop. Or, order them direct from the distributor:

The Globe Pequot Press
246 Goose Lane · P.O. Box 480 · Guilford, CT 06437-0480
www.globe-pequot.com

800-243-0495

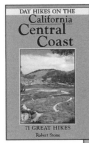

DAY HIKES ON THE
California
Central
Coast

71 GREAT HIKES
Robert Stone

DAY HIKES ON THE
California
Southern
Coast

100 GREAT HIKES
Robert Stone

DAY HIKES AROUND
MONTEREY
& CARMEL

77 GREAT HIKES
ROBERT STONE

DAY HIKES AROUND
BIG SUR

80 GREAT HIKES
ROBERT STONE

DAY HIKES IN
SAN LUIS OBISPO
COUNTY
CALIFORNIA

ROBERT STONE

DAY HIKES AROUND
SANTA
BARBARA

82 GREAT HIKES
ROBERT STONE

DAY HIKES AROUND
Ventura
County

82 GREAT HIKES
Robert Stone
2nd EDITION

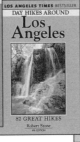

LOS ANGELES TIMES BESTSELLER
DAY HIKES AROUND
Los
Angeles

82 GREAT HIKES
Robert Stone
4th EDITION

DAY HIKES IN
YOSEMITE
NATIONAL PARK

55 GREAT HIKES
ROBERT STONE

DAY HIKES IN
SEQUOIA
AND
KINGS CANYON
NATIONAL PARKS

ROBERT STONE

DAY HIKES IN
YELLOWSTONE
NATIONAL PARK

54 GREAT HIKES
ROBERT STONE

DAY HIKES IN
Grand
Teton
NATIONAL PARK

72 GREAT HIKES
Robert Stone
4th EDITION

DAY HIKES IN THE
BEARTOOTH
MOUNTAINS

RED LODGE, MONTANA TO
YELLOWSTONE NATIONAL PARK
ROBERT STONE

DAY HIKES AROUND
BOZEMAN
MONTANA

INCLUDING THE GALLATIN
CANYON AND PARADISE VALLEY
ROBERT STONE

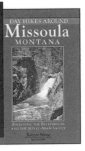

DAY HIKES AROUND
Missoula
MONTANA

INCLUDING THE BITTERROOTS
AND THE SEELEY-SWAN VALLEY
Robert Stone
2nd EDITION

DAY HIKES ON
Oahu

57 GREAT HIKES
Robert Stone
3rd EDITION

DAY HIKES ON
Maui

55 GREAT HIKES
Robert Stone
3rd EDITION

DAY HIKES ON
Kauai

55 GREAT HIKES
Robert Stone
3rd EDITION

DAY TRIPS ON
ST. MARTIN

ROBERT STONE

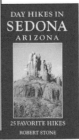

DAY HIKES IN
SEDONA
ARIZONA

25 FAVORITE HIKES
ROBERT STONE

Notes

About the Author

For more than a decade, veteran hiker Robert Stone has been writer, photographer, and publisher of Day Hike Books. Robert resides summers in the Rocky Mountains of Montana and winters on the California Central Coast. This year-round temperate climate enables him to hike throughout the year. When not hiking, Robert is researching, writing, and mapping the hikes before returning to the trails. He is an active member of OWAC (Outdoor Writers Association of California). Robert has hiked every trail in the Day Hike Book series. With over twenty hiking guides in the series, he has hiked over a thousand trails throughout the western United States and Hawaii.